"Then **Landry** Said to **Staubach**..."

The Best Dallas Cowboys Stories Ever Told

Walt Garrison
and Mark Stallard

TRIUMPH
BOOKS

Library of Congress Cataloging-in-Publication Data

Garrison, Walt.
Then Landry said to Staubach—: the best Dallas Cowboys stories ever told / Walter Garrison and Mark Stallard.
    p. cm.
 ISBN-13: 978-1-60078-022-6 (alk. paper)
 ISBN-10: 1-60078-022-9 (alk. paper)
 1. Dallas Cowboys (Football team)—History. I. Stallard, Mark, 1958–
II. Title.

 GV956.D3G37 2007
 796.332'64097642812—dc22

                                              2007020198

This book is available in quantity at special discounts for your group or organization. For further information, contact:

Triumph Books
542 South Dearborn Street
Suite 750
Chicago, Illinois 60605
(312) 939-3330
Fax (312) 663-3557

Printed in U.S.A.
ISBN: 978-1-60078-022-6
Design by Patricia Frey
Photos courtesy of AP/Wide World Photos unless otherwise indicated.

For the best boys in the world,
my sons Walt and Nate.
—M.S.

table of
contents

foreword

Probably the most famous game the Cowboys ever played was the 1967 NFL Championship Game—the Ice Bowl. Green Bay had defeated us the year before in Dallas for the championship, but when we went to Green Bay for the title game following the 1967 season, we thought we had a much better team than the Packers. When we arrived in Green Bay on Saturday, the day before the game, and went to work out, the weather was very, very nice. It was cold, but it was still 20 to 25 degrees, the sun was shining, and we said, "Oh boy, this is good." We were out there in shorts and short-sleeve shirts, working out and getting used to the cold. We thought if this was the way the weather was going to be the next day, there was no way Green Bay's old men were going to beat us.

For road games, Bob Hayes and I were roommates. Lo and behold, we woke up the next morning around 7:00 AM and heard the news: don't go outside, because it's freezing out there. It was 13 below zero, and the wind was blowing 35 to 40 miles an hour. And that just burst our bubble; a glum feeling descended over the whole team.

We weren't scared of playing them in the bitter cold—we were going to play—but it just didn't feel right. Before the game we sent a few rookies out to test the cold and check what type of shoes to wear; typical pregame stuff. They came back with tears in their eyes. They were so cold they thought they had died. In other words, it didn't matter what we did or wore, nothing was going to help protect us from the cold. We could have put on as many clothes as we wanted, all the gloves, stockings around our heads and eyes, and it wasn't going to help. When we went out to warm up before the game, we actually just stood around testing the ice on the field. We probably stayed outside all of five minutes and then went back in.

The frigid temperature at the Ice Bowl is still frozen in time and in the minds of Cowboys players and fans.

I'm not making the excuse we lost the game because it was so cold—it was cold on Green Bay's side of the field, too. Don't let them tell you it wasn't cold, because they were just as cold as we were. The field was solid ice, totally frozen. You couldn't kick dirt up. You couldn't move it. Your cleats couldn't sink into anything. It was like walking in a pair of cleats on concrete. Those were the circumstances we played under, but I believe to this day if the weather would have been decent in any other way that we would have beat them. But the cold, the frozen field, the ice and all that, that made both teams equal. And that was to Green Bay's advantage.

The game, of course, came down to the Packers' last drive— we were ahead 17–14, and I truly thought we were going to win the game. My mind-set during that last drive was, *we're going to*

stop them any minute. Green Bay got a little help from the offici-
ating, but I don't want to take anything away from them, because
that was a good drive. They went 68 yards in 12 plays, with just
under five minutes left in the game. Bart Starr, the Packers' great
quarterback, scored the winning touchdown on a quarterback
sneak. I don't know what we were expecting before that last play.
It wasn't as great a play as everybody made it out to be, because
we were standing on ice. If you're a defensive player and standing
on ice, all the offensive person has to do is touch you first and your
feet go right out from under you. I know the Packers' Jerry Kramer
made a lot of money off what was later dubbed the "greatest block
of the century," but Starr only snuck the ball for half a yard. How
great a block can you have on a half-a-yard run?

We had the better team in the Ice Bowl. The year before when
we lost to Green Bay in Dallas, we were so happy just to be in a
championship game. We played as hard as we could in that game,
but Green Bay was the better team in 1966. But in 1967, we had
the better team.

We finally got to the Super Bowl a few years later, and won it
all in Super Bowl VI. Still, the Ice Bowl remains, for me, one of the
most memorable football experiences because of what the game
was—a struggle more against the weather than the Packers.

This book is filled with many stories about the Cowboys' illustrious history. I've always been very proud to have played for the
Cowboys, and I was also lucky to have played for a Hall of Fame
coach and with so many great players, especially in a wonderful
city like Dallas.

—Cornell Green

*A five-time Pro Bowl selection at cornerback and safety, Green
played in 182 games for the Cowboys from 1962 through the
1974 season. He had the unique distinction of signing with the
Cowboys as a free agent after a three-time all-conference basketball career at Utah State. Green led the Cowboys in interceptions
four times and finished his career with 34.*

"He had the athletic skills from basketball to become a fine defensive back," Tom Landry said of Green. "His only transition was playing a sport where you could tackle someone with the ball, and Cornell never had a problem dealing with that."

Green is currently a scout for the Denver Broncos.

introduction

My absolute first memory of the Dallas Cowboys is the famous NFL Films clip of Tom Landry turning his head with his eyes closed in disappointment and despair at the end of the 1966 NFL Championship Game against the Packers. Cowboys quarterback Don Meredith, wearing Green Bay's Dave Robinson around his neck as he was being pulled to the ground, had just thrown the game-ending interception, sealing the 34–27 win—and NFL championship—for the Packers.

I've always called it Landry's losing reaction.

I must have seen that short clip hundreds of times the next five years. Whenever the Cowboys had a big game to play, there was Landry's losing grimace to remind the audience that the Cowboys had yet to win the big game. And I don't remember for sure, but CBS had to have shown that clip during the 1967 NFL Championship Game—the Ice Bowl.

The Ice Bowl was the first complete NFL game I ever watched with my dad. He wasn't that big of a Dallas fan, but he hated sports dynasties. The Yankees? No way. UCLA basketball? He did not like John Wooden. The Celtics? Not really. And the Packers, who were going for their fifth title in seven years, might have been the dynasty he liked the least.

Years later, when I read complete accounts of the 1967 NFL Championship Game and heard the players' comments on the brutally cold temperature and slashing, stabbing wind, I was a little surprised—it didn't look that bad on TV.

We cheered hard for the Cowboys, especially when Dan Reeves hit Lance Rentzel with what we hoped would be the winning touchdown pass at the beginning of the fourth quarter.

It wasn't to be. Dad took it hard, like he always did when his teams lost. But, years later, in one of the great ironic circles that life can take, the Cowboys, at least for Dad, became one of those despised dynasties.

*   *   *

If you had to pick two men in the history of the Dallas Cowboys who were responsible for the tremendous amount of success the franchise has enjoyed, you would have to start with Tom Landry and Roger Staubach. Landry's brilliant coaching, coupled with Staubach's coolheaded play and leadership, launched the Cowboys to the top and helped them stay there for most of the past 35 years.

And along the way, a few stories were told and passed along. Former Cowboys running back Walt Garrison and I compiled these stories—anecdotes primarily from the Landry-Staubach era. Walt's stories will be identified at the beginning of each chapter; the rest of the stories come from many different places and sources.

It was a lot fun putting these together. Enjoy!

chapter 1
And Then There Were Cowboys...

Jim Brown is about to be tackled by Tom Franckhauser during an October 1960 game in Dallas. Despite being challenged for professional football supremacy by the upstart AFL's Dallas Texans early in their existence, the Cowboys were always first in the hearts and minds of the locals.

You could make more money investing in government bonds, but football is more fun.
—Clint Murchison Jr., Dallas Cowboys owner, 1960–89

Doomsday

Most people think of the Dallas Cowboys of the 1960s and 1970s and think of the great offenses that we had. Exciting, point-a-minute teams. We were called "Speed Inc.," with Meredith throwing long bombs to Bob Hayes and Lance Rentzel. Don Perkins, Calvin Hill, and Duane Thomas chewed up the yards out of the backfield.

But the Dallas defense was even better than the offense. The Cowboys could always score big with Landry drawing up those plays for Meredith and Staubach. But until Tom put together that great defense we didn't win any championships.

"The Doomsday Defense," they called it. Chuck Howley, Lee Roy Jordan, Cornell Green, Mel Renfro, Charlie Waters, Cliff Harris, Jethro Pugh, and the big boy in the middle—Bob Lilly.

Of any single player from that first era of great Dallas teams, Bob Lilly had the most to do with the success of the Cowboys. Lilly was the key to the success of the Flex defense because the Flex counts on the play of one dominant tackle on the line to make it work. His job is to try to use his speed and quickness to beat the "choke" block—when the offensive guard pulls and the center tries to block back for the guard, tries to "choke" the hole.

Lilly could beat that block with ease. He was simply the quickest defensive lineman ever to play the game. Before the center could take one step, Lilly was by him. His ability to get off the line of scrimmage at the snap of the ball was awesome. The center would snap the ball and try to block Lilly and he couldn't touch him. Bob would be past him standing in the other team's backfield. A lot of times Lilly would get to the quarterback before he had time to hand off to the running back.

So they couldn't pull the guard on Lilly because it was like an invitation for Bob to cream the quarterback. That eliminates about 40 percent of a team's offense right there.

Lilly made the Flex possible, which made our defense great. Most 4-3 linemen sat back and tried to read the offense. But in the Flex, Lilly's job was to create havoc. He had to control his gap, but as soon as something happened, he could take off. And Lilly was awesome at screwing up an offense before it could get out of its tracks. —W.G.

The Birth of the Cowboys

The Dallas Cowboys were born in 1960 when the NFL, with the blessing of George Halas of the Chicago Bears, sold Clint Murchison a franchise for the then-whopping sum of $600,000.

The Cowboys got most of their players in a special expansion draft in which Dallas got to choose three players from each of the other NFL teams. But first those teams were allowed to "freeze" the top 25 players on their rosters. The Cowboys picked over what was left—a bunch of marginal players with little talent, serviceable players on the downside of their careers, or the "attitude" guys.

And the NFL gave Landry and his staff all of 24 hours to make selections.

What were the early days of the Cowboys like? Not good. The team offices were in a room shared by an auto club. Practices were held at Burnett Field, an old baseball diamond. The players weren't the only ones using the lockers at this cockroach den. They'd come back from practice and find rats had eaten the tongues out of their shoes. When they'd shower, scorpions would scoot across the shower floor.

The early Cowboys teams weren't just bad, they were awful. They didn't win a game the first year. In the 11th game of the season, they managed a tie with the New York Giants, 31–31, and they tore the locker room apart celebrating.

In a 1962 game against the Steelers, Cowboys quarterback Eddie LeBaron threw a 99-yard touchdown bomb to Frank Clarke. But Dallas guard Andy Cvercko was caught holding in the end zone. According to the rules, the other team is awarded a safety when a hold is committed in your own end zone. So the longest TD in Cowboys history was wiped out, and Pittsburgh got two points.

Tom Landry is greeted at the airport in Dallas by general manager Tex Schramm on December 28, 1959.

The 1961 Dallas Cowboys coaching staff. From left to right are assistant coaches Brad Ecklund, Tom Dahms, and Babe Dimancheff. Tom Landry is kneeling.

In 1961, Dallas beat the Giants in New York and it made their year. They were 4-9-1. In 1962 they won five games, but in 1963, after being tabbed by *Sports Illustrated* as the team to beat in their division, they had only four victories. In 1964, they were back up to five wins, with eight losses and a tie.

But Landry was slowly building his team. He had a stud at quarterback in Don Meredith, and Bob Lilly was a force at defensive tackle, but there just weren't enough other good players to help those guys out.

In 1965, things started to turn around. That year's rookie crop was one of the best in Cowboys history. First they landed Craig Morton, a quarterback from California with a .45-caliber arm, who would eventually lead the club to two Super Bowls. Dallas also got Ralph Neely, an offensive tackle from Oklahoma, who was All-Pro for the next decade; Bob Hayes, the fastest man in the solar system; plus Jethro Pugh, Dan Reeves, and Jerry Rhome.

Dallas promptly started to win some games. They ended up 7-7 in 1965, finished second in their division, and got a trip to the Runner-up Bowl in Miami.

From 1966 through 1969, Dallas continued to draft quality players, and the winning snowballed. In 1966, the Cowboys were 10-3-1 and played Green Bay for the NFL championship. And the winning never stopped. The Cowboys went 21 straight years without a losing season.

Two Teams, Too Many

The prospect of Dallas having a successful professional football team was not always a foregone conclusion. After failing miserably to support a pro team in 1952, the city found itself in the peculiar position of having *two* professional football teams in 1960.

There were the NFL-expansion Rangers, who just a few weeks into existence changed their name to the Cowboys, and the Dallas Texans of the newly formed American Football League. The duel for the heart of the city pitted local millionaires against each other:

37-year-old Clint Murchison Jr. of the Cowboys, and AFL founder Lamar Hunt, who was just 28.

The Cowboys-Texans rivalry mirrored the larger struggle between the NFL and the AFL, which filed and lost an antitrust suit against the longer-established league. The rivals competed to sign college prospects, insulted each other, wooed fans in different ways, sold a few tickets, gave away a *lot* of tickets, and tried not to lose too much money.

When it appeared that neither team would win a solid fan base any time soon, Murchison proposed a mock settlement to Hunt.

"We'll flip a coin," he said. "The winner gets to leave town."

The duel in Dallas finally ended when Hunt saw the future with realistic eyes: his team would die first in a long war with the NFL Cowboys. So, following the 1962 "championship" season—the Cowboys won five games that year—Hunt moved his franchise to Kansas City for the 1963 season.

Dallas belonged to the Cowboys.

Building a Winner

It took time, but after the first few seasons, the Cowboys slowly started finding the pieces to field a winning team.

"We were putting together a lot of free agents and people who weren't supposed to be big enough, like Lee Roy Jordan, and people who weren't supposed to be able to hold the ball, like Mel Renfro, and basketball players, like Cornell Green, and track guys, like Bob Hayes and Mike Gaechter," Bob Lilly said of the Cowboys' growth into a winning team. "Getting Ralph Neely, through a series of breaks, was very important. See, he had signed with Houston, which was then in the other league [the rival American Football League], but he really wanted to play for us and so he signed with Dallas, too. That went to court, and he was awarded to the Cowboys, but after the two leagues merged [1966], I think we gave the Oilers something in the draft the next year to make the deal official. Ralph became a very integral part of our team."

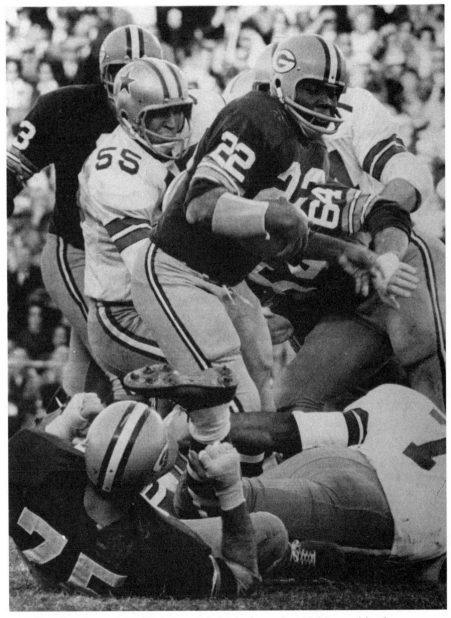

The Cowboys steadily improved throughout the 1960s and broke through with their first winning season in 1966 before losing to the Green Bay Packers and Elijah Pitts (22) in the NFL Championship Game in Dallas.

As Landry assembled his team, the wins came more frequently.

"In the beginning, we had a lot of trouble stopping the good teams," Lilly said. "We had a hard time with Cleveland and Jimmy Brown, Green Bay and Paul Hornung. The New York Giants always gave us trouble, and because Coach Landry had played and coached there, he always tried a little harder, walked around all week just a little more intense…and we paid a little more of a price if we lost to them. It was a slow, slow process, but eventually we learned what he wanted, and he got together the kind of players he needed. Suddenly, we had our defense and the people to play it."

The Loser Bowl

"Nineteen sixty-five was a big year for us," Lee Roy Jordan said of the Cowboys' first non-losing season. "We ended up 7–7 and beat some good opponents, such as the Giants and the Steelers. And we ended up going to what they called 'the Loser Bowl' back then, played by the two division runner-ups." The game was actually called the Playoff Bowl, and proceeds went to the players' retirement fund.

"We played the Colts in a little playoff game down in Miami," Jordan said. "We didn't play too good, but we sure had a good time in going. That was the turning point for the Cowboys in making us realize that we had a lot of talent and that with experience we could be a good football team. It took us a long time, but we finally did prove that, after struggling through some great seasons in which we were unable to win it all, like when we lost to the Green Bay Packers in the playoffs in two consecutive years."

Naming Rights

"I named the team," Cowboys president and general manager Tex Schramm said of the franchise's name selection. "I did the logo and picked the colors. Before we got the franchise, we planned to name the team the Dallas Steers. But after thinking about it, nobody liked the idea of a castrated bull." Of course, that's what the team played like its first few years.

"So we decided to name them the Dallas Rangers," Schramm continued. "Rangers was a good name; it embodied the state. But then there was a professional [minor league] baseball team calling itself the Dallas Rangers. Clint was leaving for vacation in the Bahamas—he said, 'Well, you make this decision.' So he took off, and I named them the Cowboys."

While the Country Cried, They Had to Play

As the country mourned the assassination of President John F. Kennedy on November 22, 1963, the NFL's top man, Pete Rozelle, made arguably the toughest decision of his career—the NFL would play all games that weekend.

The Cowboys were in Cleveland for a game that suddenly had no meaning. None of the other 13 NFL teams that played on Sunday, November 24, 1963, carried the stigma that was now attached to Dallas, the city where Kennedy had been assassinated two days before.

"We felt like we were some real hated bastards," Cowboys fullback Don Perkins said. "The sentiment was that Dallas had killed the president. It wasn't a good time to be a Dallas Cowboy...We felt the whole country indicting us."

The Cowboys knew they were being viewed differently by the people of Cleveland the night before the game.

"I didn't blame people for being mad at us," Bob Lilly said. "I think I probably would've felt the same way."

In a 1982 interview, Don Meredith, the Cowboys' starting quarterback, described hearing a haunting sound as his team made its way through a tunnel, through the visiting dugout, and onto the field. Stepping onto the field, Meredith realized the sound he heard was the pounding footsteps of 400 servicemen during a pregame ceremony in honor of the late president.

"Here we come out, the Dallas Cowboys, with our stars on our hats," Meredith told Michael Granberry, now a reporter for the *Dallas Morning News*. "And it was like going to the lions with the Christians."

"We were really kind of worried about getting killed," Lilly said of playing in Cleveland. "We stood there going, 'I wonder if there are any snipers around here?' We wore our helmets the whole time and wore those big parkas."

Meredith had a poor game, throwing two interceptions and fumbling once as the Cowboys lost, 27–17.

"I can remember we were really in no frame of mind to play a ballgame," Meredith said. "It was really a listless game, and I'll never forget that."

Frank Clarke, a receiver on that Cowboys team, has no memory of the game.

"I wasn't really there," Clarke said. "I don't even remember how I did."

"It wasn't much fun the rest of that year," Lilly said of the 1963 season. "It kind of killed our [spirit]. You know, we tried and went out and went through our motions. But I don't think we had it. I think the assassination affected the Cowboys for at least another year, as far as feeling guilty about our city. Dallas was kind of a coming star and then all of a sudden it was tarnished. It took Dallas a long time to get over it. It didn't take the team quite as long. Meredith and I, as Texans, probably felt it a little more. Coach Landry, too. We were kind of ashamed of our city. It's not the best mentality for playing football. Somehow, emotionally, it did something."

chapter 2
The Coach–Tom Landry

Tom Landry, pictured here in July 1961, faced an uphill climb in building the team.

Landry was a great football coach.
You can pick on his weaknesses, but you
have to look at history. Over a long period,
what he did was pretty darn good.

—Roger Staubach

Landry—The Coach

I'll tell you something about Landry: I never met a more caring guy in my life, but he was all business on game day. During the week, he'd crack a joke every once in a while when he thought things were funny, but he was usually all work. On Sunday he concentrated on the game. Dan Reeves said something that made probably the most sense about Coach Landry. Reeves said, "You know, I always wondered why Coach Landry never smiled and never got into the game. I mean, when a play was over it was over. He didn't jump up on a good play or get disappointed on a bad play."

Dan says that when he first went to Denver and was coaching up there and standing on the sideline, he would get too much into the play he'd called rather than worry about the next play: "You know I'd be arguing and looking at what happened out there and trying to figure out what went wrong or right. Then I'd look up and there'd be only 10 seconds left on the play clock and I wouldn't have time left to call a play and I'd have to call a timeout. So I learned to be like Coach Landry. Once you call a play, that's it. There's nothing else you can do."

So he started thinking like, *If this play works and it's second and four, what am I gonna call? If it doesn't work, and it's second and nine, what am I gonna do?* He put his head in the game the way Coach Landry did. That's what good coaches do. They think ahead and don't worry about the play that's going on now, because you can't do anything about it. Good or bad, you can't do anything about it.

Coach Landry gave some pep talks before games. And he would chew you out pretty good at halftime if you weren't doing your job. But if I had one word to describe Coach Landry, it would be *fair.* He was a fair coach. If you were better than the guy that was playing ahead of you, then you would be in there; and if you weren't, you wouldn't.

I don't think Coach Landry ever got close to any players. After I retired, my wife and I went into a restaurant, and Landry and his wife came in. And he said, "Hey Walt, you come over and sit with us. We went over and sat with them and visited, and then he picked up the check. And I told him, "Coach, you've never said this many words to me in nine years." He said, "Walt, you can't get close to players when you're coaching while they're playing, because if I become friends with the players, it might change the way I look at them as football players, and it might alter the team decisions that I need to make." Which makes a lot of sense. He didn't want to be close to you while you were playing, because he didn't want to keep a guy he liked over a guy who might have been a better football player. –W.G.

"Three Times, At Least"

If people had a hard time figuring out Landry's system, it was nothing compared with the trouble they had trying to figure out his personality.

A reporter once asked me if I'd ever seen Tom Landry smile.

"No," I answered, "I only played nine years. But I know he smiled at least three times, because he's got three kids."

The image of the Dallas Cowboys is of this impersonal, cold machine. All business and no warmth. Nobody cares about anything except winning and losing. This image stems directly from Coach Landry's demeanor on the sidelines on Sunday. The TV cameras catch him prowling the sidelines with that blocked hat and chiseled profile right out of *Dick Tracy*. Whether the Cowboys are winning or losing, whether they just scored a big touchdown or turned the ball over inside their own 10-yard line, his expression and manner never change. But let me tell you, it's a misleading image.

A coach has to really discipline himself not to get caught up emotionally in the game. And that's hard to do because football is an exciting game. It gets you excited playing it or watching it. And coaches are human, too. They'd love to scream for a big touchdown run.

It's not a personality flaw in Landry that he shows no emotion on the sidelines. He's not cold. He's under control. He'd love to go nuts, but if he wants to do what's best for the team, if he wants to win, he can't.

They say football is a game of emotion, but Landry didn't encourage you to be emotional on the field. But he didn't discourage it, either. Landry wasn't big on pep talks. His approach was to do whatever he thought was necessary to get ready for the game and get the players ready. He would teach you everything there was to know about your opponent that week and give you a game plan that would beat that opponent. He figured if you did your job, you'd win. And your job was to play football. So if he had to give you a pep talk to get you to do your job, then you shouldn't be there.

Every once in a long while he'd chew us out a little at halftime if we had really played lousy. But most of the time if things weren't going right he'd come in at the half and try and fix it. If the offense was having trouble, he'd go in and meet with the offense. "They didn't do exactly what we thought, so let's do this." And he'd get out the chalkboard and draw up some plays.

Sometimes if we were really stinking up the field he might come in and say, "The game plan is good. You're just not executing."

But he never yelled, "Kill! Win! Kill!"   —W.G.

The Genius

It wasn't an accident that Dallas was so successful. The Cowboys had a plan, and the chief architect of that plan was Tom Landry. We're talking about a very smart boy here, folks. This guy could have been just about anything he wanted, because he had a ferocious will to win and brains leaking out his ears.

They throw the word *genius* around pretty loosely these days. But that's what Landry is. Most of us are copiers. And if you're a really smart guy, you figure out what the best things are and why they're the best and you use them. You copy.

Landry's a couple light years ahead of that. He's the kind of guy who invents the stuff that the rest of us copy. He looked at football the way it was being played at the time, and he devised completely new systems on offense *and* defense to beat that game. And for the past 20 years, the rest of the league has been trying to understand and then copy what Landry invented.

That's genius.

Landry invented the Flex defense out of thin air. He designed it. He developed it. He choreographed it. He did it all. When Tom was the young defensive coordinator for the Giants, they played a simple 4-3 defense. Then Tom's mind got churning, and before long the Flex defense was a reality.

The Flex defense is simply an undershifted or overshifted defensive line. If you were flexed strong, you'd line up in a 4-3 but really you were going to play an overshifted defense. When you were flexed weak, you'd line up in a 4-3 but you were really playing an undershifted defense.

The advantage was that you could play a lot of different defenses and get it all to look the same to your opponent. The quarterback would get up to the line of scrimmage, see a 4-3 defense lined up in front of him, call an audible to beat it, and at the snap of the ball, everything suddenly changed. Each player in the Flex had to learn to read keys from the action of the offensive players and then react with a move that Landry figured to be the most effective in that situation. The defense was dependent on players going to an assigned area and "holding." The theory being that if every man was in the proper place, the offense went nowhere.

See, the Flex is a gap-control defense. The offensive theory back then was headed by Vince Lombardi's "run to daylight" offense. They'd give the ball to the running back, and when he'd see a hole open, a little daylight, he'd break for it. He'd run to daylight.

With the gap defense, the defensive man would plug up the holes and there wasn't any daylight to run to. The only problem is, it's a very disciplined system. If somebody doesn't do his job, the

Landry directs his players through a final workout in December 1971 before a playoff game against Minnesota.

coordination of the whole thing will be broken and there will be daylight all over the place. Players can lose confidence in it easily. You can see some gaping holes in the Flex because when your linemen fill up the gaps, you no longer have players lined up equally spaced out. There might be 20 feet between defensive linemen.

The key to the Flex was to have a bunch of good football players who didn't make mistakes—people who were disciplined enough to play their position and smart enough to know what they were supposed to do. –W.G.

The Genius, Part 2

Landry and Hank Stram of the Kansas City Chiefs are usually credited with the development of the multiple-set offense. But nobody, including Kansas City, used the multiple-set with as much variation or as much success.

Landry developed his offense by looking at it from a defensive point of view. He noted what caused his own defense the most problems and went from there.

He had always felt that one of the easiest teams to defend against was a team that just sat there in one or two formations. What caused fits was a team that gave you a lot of different looks—different formations and lots of movement—an offense that constantly forced you to make adjustments even as the play was getting under way.

If you were gonna run just a basic set offense, you had to have great athletes. You had to have a team like the Green Bay Packers of the 1960s. A huge line with a couple of Hall of Fame running backs behind it, like Jim Taylor and Paul Hornung. Green Bay just said, "Here we come. Stop us if you can." And nobody could, because their players were so great.

But in those early years in Dallas great players were scarce. Landry knew that the only way to move the ball with the talent he had was to outsmart everybody else. He felt that with the multiple-set offense he could move the football and score points with less talent. And, of course, if and when he came up with some really talented players, Dallas could run wild using the same concept. And that's exactly what happened.

In 1966 the Cowboys scored 445 points in only 14 games, a record that held up until 1980 when they scored 454 points in a 16-game schedule and came back and scored 479 in 1983. That's puttin' some points on the board!

Before Landry came along, coaches used shifts and different formations, but nobody did what Landry did. Nobody at that time was also shifting the line, blocking the view of the defense so they couldn't see what we were up to in the backfield. Every play was a surprise. After a while they didn't know what was coming at them. Confusion reigned like turds at a horse show.

It's hard enough to stop a good offense when you know what they're up to. But when you haven't got a clue what they're gonna do next, it's devastating. That was the trademark of the Dallas teams. They had no trademark. You could never say, "Oh, Dallas loves to pass or run." They did it all from every position and formation.

Again, the problem was you had to have players who could understand what the hell Landry was talking about. Meredith had a good line: "I took a page of Landry's play book to a Chinese laundry and they gave me three shirts and a pillowcase."

The Cowboys used to give IQ tests to prospects, and if they didn't score high enough, the team wouldn't touch them. The Cowboys just didn't draft a player unless his intelligence level was high. They always looked at physical skills, but if a player didn't have it upstairs, he couldn't cut it at Dallas, because you had a goddamn intellectual devising the game plan. It was like having Socrates as your coach. Year after year we had guys who came in with talent to burn, but they couldn't make the team because they couldn't learn the system. The guy could run a 4.4/40, but if he couldn't understand the playbook, he wasn't gonna do Landry much good. –W.G.

To Start With, Nothing

"I made a real plea to the NFL owners that we were going into Dallas, fighting another league, and we needed players, we needed help," Landry said of how the Cowboys were first assembled. "I was at my best. They said, 'We will help you.' Every team would protect all but eight of their players, and we would get three off each team. Every time we picked one, they could protect one. That's the way we started."

Of course, it wasn't much to start with.

"We started with nothing," Landry said of his first roster of players. "One of the players I remember from those years was

Landry shouts from the sideline during a game against the Los Angeles Rams in December 1980. The Cowboys won the NFC wild-card game by a score of 34–13.

Eddie LeBaron. The worst thing I ever did for Eddie was talk him out of being a lawyer in Midland. I guarantee you those guys took a beating. I hate to say those teams were awful, because it would be a discredit to those guys. But we were weak. We just didn't have enough personnel."

Favorite Years

To an extent, it's hard to imagine Tom Landry reminiscing about his past teams. Since he was always a coach who moved forward and tried very hard not to look backward, he was able to cut loose players in an unemotional way. Landry's manner of always focusing on the future makes the memories he does share all the more enlightening.

Landry recalled of speedy receiver Bob Hayes, "When Bobby came into the league…he had that great year in 1966, which was our first great year. I mean, he'd just kill anybody in man-to-man coverage. He was just awesome. We'd go to multiple sets and he was gone, nobody could stay with him. Meredith said he was the only receiver he couldn't overthrow.

"You know, with Meredith and Hayes, and the defense coming into its own…'65 and '66 were favorite years of mine…we had some great times…because it was the first time this city became turned on to football. And once they were, they expected it all over again; they became complacent, and we had to put ourselves into that pressure every year, to try to make the people get what they want. It was, I think, a large part of why we were so successful, because everybody expected it and you just don't want to disappoint them."

It isn't surprising that Landry, like almost everyone else associated with the team, felt the Cowboys should have won the Ice Bowl.

"That first one [championship game], the one in '66, that was really exciting," Landry said. "We almost beat Green Bay twice. Of course, we weren't the experienced club they were, but we had great games against them. The one up in Green Bay, no question, we should have won. That ice game. They just pulled together with their great experience, their character.

"If we had won that game, see, it would have changed the whole psyche of the team. I think that's true. People started writing, started saying, that we couldn't win the big games, and right after that second Packer game, we really bombed in two games against Cleveland [the 1968 and 1969 divisional playoff games]...we really bombed."

Staubach on Landry

"Coach Landry was an industrial engineer; so he was very organized and always spent a lot of time on preparation," said Staubach. "And he had goals that were outstanding—reasonable goals, believable and achievable—and he measured them as a coach. I think that's why he had a 20-year winning streak. It was through preparation. I've really believed in business that you have to work hard, you have to be prepared, and you have to develop a consistency, which he taught me. Plus, you have to do things right. He was a person—you read about him, but he's even better than that. He taught me a lot about walking your talk and living your life and doing the right thing. And he knew the game of football, and he had us well prepared. In business, you also have to make sure you're working hard and prepare yourself for the things you have to do."

Work Ethic

Walt Garrison was in awe of the long hours Tom Landry put in to prepare his team.

"Landry was a hell of a coach," Garrison said. "His work ethic was unbelievable. Some people think that coaches just show up and coach and that's it. Coach Landry would work 18- to 20-hour days. The average fan doesn't understand how hard coaches work. They're there at 6:00 in the morning and don't go home until 6:00 at night. And then they do work stuff when they get home. It's a stupid way to make a living, but you gotta love it."

Acceptance

It took a while—four years—before the scars of his firing in 1989 by the Cowboys' new owner, Jerry Jones, had healed properly and Tom Landry was able to take his place among the other Cowboys greats.

"I think it would be foolish for me to say I am not going to go into the Ring of Honor because I am mad at Jerry or somebody else," Landry said after finally accepting Jones's invitation. "That is foolishness, because I am not at all. It was never a problem with any feelings I had towards the new management and the football team. The thing that hurts me the most is when people say that I'm unforgiving with Jerry and all. That never entered my mind from the time I got out of football, because I was really looking to get out of football at the time. The move didn't bother me, really, too much. I guess Jerry and I would agree that maybe we could have done it a little differently."

chapter 3
The Ice Bowl

Both teams as well as the fans endured bitter cold temperatures in a game that came to be known as the Ice Bowl.
Photograph courtesy of Corbis.

I remember the first play vividly.
The referee blew his whistle, and it froze
on his lip. He pulled part of his lip off,
and the blood froze down his chin.

—Bob Lilly, on the Ice Bowl

Glad I Wasn't Really Playing

The field was exactly like playing on an ice rink. I mean literally. It was one big solid piece of ice. You couldn't stand up, much less run and cut. Guys would be standing on the sidelines minding their own business, and they'd shift their feet and the next thing they knew, they were on their asses.

"We must be crazy to be out here playing," I said to Don Perkins.

"We're not crazy," he said. "Look behind you. There's about 50,000 crazy sonuvabitches up there. They paid to come out here and freeze to death."

In the end, it turned out to be an exciting football game. It was a close, defensive struggle. The Packers dominated the game early, jumping ahead 14–0, just like they had the previous year. Then [defensive end] George Andrie picked up a fumble and ran it in and that got us started, 14–7. A little later the Packers' Willie Wood fumbled a punt return at their 17 and [Danny] Villanueva kicked a field goal.

We trailed 14–10 at the half.

Nobody did a thing on offense in the third quarter. Then, on the first play of the fourth quarter, Reeves threw a halfback-option pass for a touchdown that put us ahead. Between quarters Meredith had come up to Dan and asked, "What about the half-back pass?" We'd been running the quick pitch a lot, and their safeties were really coming up to stop it. That left somebody open downfield.

So Reeves kept his hands down in his jock through the quarter to keep his hands warm. And when they broke the huddle to run that play, Reeves kept them right next to his jewels, proba-bly the warmest place in Green Bay that day. He took his hands out of his jock at the last second and it worked. Reeves lofted a pass to a wide-open Lance Rentzel, who almost fell on his ass as he skated and slipped into the end zone.

Dallas was ahead, 17–14.

On the next series Green Bay went nowhere, and then we kept the ball for 10 minutes on a long drive. When the Packers finally got the ball back, they were on their 32-yard line with four and a half minutes to play. No one thought they had a chance to drive the length of the field in that weather. But they did it. They moved steadily downfield to our 30. Then Chuck Howley slipped and went down covering Chuck Mercein and, just like that, they were down to our 11. Three plays later they were on our 2, first and goal. They tried a couple off-tackle plays and got nowhere. With 16 seconds left in the game, still trailing by three, they took their last timeout.

Everybody figured with no timeouts they'd probably go for a field goal to tie the game. Or they could try a pass into the end zone and if it was incomplete, the clock would stop and they could kick the field goal. But a run didn't figure at all. *If they don't make it, the game's over and we win.* A quarterback sneak by Bart Starr is just not the smart play.

So that's what they do, and he scores to win the game.

Green Bay's Jerry Kramer writes a book called *Instant Replay* about how he made the key block on Jethro Pugh and it turns out to be the best-selling football book of all time and it makes Kramer famous and a million dollars.

And we lose another heartbreaker.

If Bart Starr doesn't score, if Jethro Pugh stuffs Kramer, then Jethro could have written the best seller. If, if, if.

Like Meredith used to say, "If ifs and buts were candies and nuts, we'd all have a Merry Christmas." –W.G.

It's Hard

Losing the Ice Bowl was pretty disappointing. Of course, it wasn't for me because that was like my second year in the league and I was still glad to be part of the team, because I wasn't starting or anything. But that was a big disappointment. I could tell from the veterans that it was big disappointment for a lot of them. We lost the Super Bowl and that was a big disappointment because that was a game we should have won and we didn't.

So anytime you have an opportunity to win a Super Bowl and you don't, it's always a disappointment. But for a lot of the guys on the team, losing that '67 championship game to Green Bay was really hard to get over. –W.G.

It Hurt

As much of a letdown as the loss to the Packers had been in the 1966 Championship Game, nothing compares to losing the Ice Bowl for the Cowboys.

"That game hurt more than the first loss to Green Bay the year before," Tom Landry said. "The first one, we weren't in their league. We were down 14–0 before we ever touched the ball. The next game, I think we were a better football team.

"That Ice Bowl game...Lombardi had put heaters under the field, and we were really looking forward to that game. It wasn't predicted to be that cold; it was 20 when we got there the day before. We stayed in a motel in Green Bay where the doors opened to the outside. I remember going to bed and getting up for breakfast in the morning, and I couldn't believe it. Everything was ice. It was like the North Pole. You can imagine the shock. I think we were in shock most of the game. [Minority owner] Toddie Lee Wynne had this big coat he gave me. I would have frozen to death if he didn't give it to me. Boy, it was freezing."

Frostbite

"Everyone says there are some things in your life you never forget, and one was when our president was shot, and another was the Ice Bowl," Bob Lilly said of his playing days. "I may have forgotten a lot of other things, but I will never forget the Ice Bowl.

"Lombardi had installed a system of pipes underneath the ground that were warmed by water going through them, and the day before the game we went to the stadium to work out. The field was in good shape, though just a little bit damp. You could wear real cleats. The turf was pretty good, and temperature was nice, the wind wasn't blowing, just a pretty day, and when we warmed up we didn't even feel the cold at all so we were all happy.

"We all knew a cold front was coming, but it wasn't supposed to get there until after the game, sometime the next night. So we weren't concerned about that.

"The next morning George Andrie, my roommate, got up, and went to Mass at about 6:30 or 7:00 AM, and he came back about 7:30 AM. I was up, watching TV. He came in and didn't say a word. We were in a Holiday Inn. He got a glass of water, and threw the water on the plate-glass window. Half the water froze before it got down to the windowsill. He said, 'Bob, it's cold. It's already 10 below, and there's about a 35-mile-an-hour wind out. It's sup-posed to be 20 below by game time.'"

The effect on the team was immense.

"We were pretty somber at breakfast," Lilly said. "We went on out to the field, got dressed, and as we were going to go out and warm up, Andrie said, 'You and I are going to have to be leaders out there today. I grew up in this weather,' and he talked me into not wearing any long-handles or any warm-up jacket, because we were going to show these guys that it wasn't that bad. And so I walked out that door, and when I did, I said to myself, 'You fool, you fool.' I looked at George, and I said, 'Don't ever ask me to do anything like this again.' I like froze to death. I had icicles hanging out my nose about four inches. And I was absolutely freezing. I just barely got through warm-ups.

"We went back into the locker room, and I put on everything I had. I got my long-handles out, put Saran Wrap on my feet, put an extra pair of socks on. [Assistant coach] Ernie Stautner wouldn't let us wear gloves. Ernie said, 'Men don't wear gloves in this league.' We went back out and every guy on Green Bay had

As evidenced by this Boyd Dowler catch of a Bart Starr touchdown pass, the Packers adjusted to the bitter cold temperatures better than Mel Renfro and the Cowboys.

gloves on, and as a result we all got frostbite. I didn't get much, but we all got frostbite. And we about froze to death.

"The field wasn't totally frozen when we started, but by the first quarter I had already taken my cleats off and put on my soccer shoes. We were starting to slide around. I was really having a field day then because Gale Gillingham had on his cleats, and he was trying to figure out what was going on, because I was getting around him so fast. So he put on his soccer shoes, and by the time the end of the game came, we were on a solid sheet of ice, all the way from the 20-yard line in."

Somewhere Else

For the players who ventured onto Green Bay's frozen turf to play the Ice Bowl, the pregame experiences were similar, but still different. Don Perkins, like all of his teammates, will never forget the horrible, blasting cold the Cowboys faced on December 31, 1967.

"The day before the game, they had heating coils on the field to warm the field," Perkins recalled. "When we practiced on Saturday, it was 26 or 28 degrees, and that was fine. We could handle that. We could get traction, which was important because we had a fast team. We felt good because the playing conditions were okay."

George Andrie picks up a Bart Starr fumble and is about to follow teammate Jethro Pugh (75) into the end zone for the Cowboys' first score in the Ice Bowl.

It wasn't okay. The next morning it was 15 below zero. Perkins couldn't believe it. So overwhelming was the cold that the window in their room was frosted over. "I don't think I felt overly intimidated by the weather because everyone had to play in it, so I was like, just shut up and do it," Perkins said. "I don't think you get used to playing in weather like that, but I grew up playing in cold weather in Iowa. In New Mexico, we played teams up and down the Rocky Mountains, and we played schools in Montana, so I knew about cold weather. They had heaters and blowers on the sideline, but the guys not playing were really freezing because we all know you get colder standing around than when you're running around and moving. We'd come off the field, and the biggest battle we had was getting all of the backups away from the heaters because they weren't giving up their spaces.

"We were slipping and sliding all day, and I didn't pick up a whole lot of yards. It really didn't matter what I did because we lost the game. As an athlete and competitor, that's how you feel after the game. The object is to win the game, and if we didn't do that, then what I did didn't matter. It was like a morgue in the locker room after the game. I can still see Bob Lilly and Jethro Pugh with their heads down. I don't remember any comment from Coach Landry. I just remember that long plane ride. Everybody was trying to be somewhere else and wishing they were someone else."

A Heartfelt Dandy

Following the loss to the Packers in the Ice Bowl, CBS's Frank Gifford thought it would be good if the network could interview a few players on the losing team. It didn't take much coaxing from Gifford to corral Don Meredith, who agreed to talk about the game to the national television audience.

"Don, you came so close," Gifford said to Meredith. "How does it feel to lose this one?"

"The way I look at it, we really didn't lose it," Meredith responded. He was emotionally drained from the game, and his blood-stained T-shirt showed the fatigue and hurt he was feeling.

"Dadgummit, we didn't lose anything."

Meredith choked a little on his words then, and poured out his heart to Gifford and the TV audience. He told the world how proud he was of his teammates, how hard they had played that day, and how he blamed himself for the loss.

He felt just awful for his team.

chapter 4
Dandy Don

Even when he was off the field Don Meredith, shown here on the sideline during a 1963 game against the Philadelphia Eagles, seemed to draw attention. Photograph courtesy of Corbis.

Meredith was like nobody else they
ever had in Dallas. Or probably ever will.
In a word, Joe Don was cool.

—Walt Garrison

Joe Don

Meredith was a true celebrity, and there weren't many real celebrities in football—a guy who could hold the spotlight even when he wasn't on the field. Joe Namath was a celebrity. Broadway Joe. He was single and good-looking, so all the unmarried women and most of the married ones loved him. He owned a bar, and he was a great football player. He told everybody he was going to beat the world champion Colts in Super Bowl III, and he went out and did it. That's the kind of stuff charisma is made of.

Roger Staubach was a celebrity too, but for exactly the opposite reasons as Namath. He wasn't flashy. He was cut from the military cloth. "Yes, sir." "No, sir." He was the family, go-to-church type which a lot of people relate to. And he was exciting as hell to watch. –W.G.

The Quarterback

Roger Staubach got mad at me one time. They asked me who was the best quarterback I ever played with, and I said, "Don Meredith." And Joe Don was—he was the smartest quarterback and had a lot of ability. I mean he was a great quarterback. Craig Morton had the best arm. If you had one game to win, I'd go with Roger because Roger was a winner. Meredith was too, he just didn't have any help—he had a little help, but he didn't have a lot of help. He was getting better when he retired. Meredith was just a little ahead of his time. He took us to two championship playoff games when we weren't that good.

He was a heck of a quarterback, a heck of a leader. You could always tell when Meredith came into a room. He was the center of attention and that's the way he liked it. And everybody looked up to him to lead. I mean offense, defense, everybody.

Meredith was the man.

You want to go beer drinking? All right, where's Joe Don going? Let's go with him. It was that kind of deal. And he was a great quarterback. –W.G.

Meredith, coming back from broken ribs, suits up for a Cowboys workout in October 1967. Photograph courtesy of Corbis.

"Sing a Song"

At training camp the veteran players always make the rookies get up and sing. Meredith got me up. He'd say, "Get up and sing, rookie." Well, okay. He'd say, "Sing your alma mater." Well, Oklahoma State's alma mater ain't got no words. It's just music, you know. So I sang, I don't know, I'm a big country music fan, so I sang "Waltz Across Texas" or something. I don't remember. One of them old beer-drinking songs.

Most of the time when you're a rookie you have to sing once, maybe twice. Meredith had me sing every night for 10 days. In the end, when I started thinking if it was a song he knew, he and Buddy Dial would get up and sing with me. It turned out to be better than I thought because Meredith kind of took me under his wing and he would mess with me, but he wouldn't let anybody else mess with me, which was pretty cool.
–W.G.

The 1966 NFL Championship Game

Meredith never let his teammates get tight. Especially before a big game. The night before the NFL Championship Game against Green Bay in 1966, word got around that Meredith was hurt. The game the next day was not only for the title but for the right to go to Super Bowl I.

We always had a team meeting the night before a game at the hotel where we were staying. And when I got to the meeting that night everything's very quiet. It's like a morgue.

I sat down and somebody whispered to me, "You see what happened to Meredith?"

"No."

"He went through a plate-glass window when he was out shopping today."

"What!?"

"He cut himself up real bad and he's not gonna be able to play tomorrow."

Meredith comes in about that time and sits down. You could see he was completely dejected. His head's hung down real low. And there was this big bloody scar across his face. It was gruesome. My heart just stopped when I saw him because our chances of winning suddenly weren't very good anymore.

Coach Landry got up and made his talk, told us what we had to do to win the ball game. When he got through, Meredith got up and we all figured he was gonna give us a little talk about how we could win the game without him or some other bullshit we wouldn't believe.

And, yank! He just peeled this ugly bloody scar off his face. He'd had some Hollywood makeup guy he knew come in and put the damn thing on him. It looked so real you wanted to throw up when you looked at it.

The whole place just exploded with laughter. Sigmund Freud couldn't have done a better job of relaxing us. Here we were, a young expansion team, first time in the playoffs, and we were going to face Lombardi's Packers. And Meredith just turned it all into a big joke. And the next day we went out and played a hell of a ballgame. –W.G.

Rookie's Night Out

The night before a game during my rookie season, I was lying up in my hotel room and Meredith called me up and said, "Walt, what're you doing for supper tonight?"

Well, the truth was I wanted to rest up. I'd been playing behind Don Perkins, so just about all my playing that year consisted of running up and down the field covering kicks. But we'd clinched the division the week before, and I figured Landry ain't gonna take a chance of hurting Perkins in a meaningless game, and I'd get my shot to show what I could do.

So I told Meredith, "Oh, I think I'll get some room service, watch a little TV, and get to bed early."

"No, you're not," Meredith ordered. "Be down in the lobby in 30 minutes."

Now a rookie in those days did not question a veteran, especially not Meredith. Don was the bona fide team leader of the Cowboys on and off the field. So I got up, dressed, and went downstairs. When I walked into the lobby, Meredith was standing there wearing a chauffeur's cap. Somehow he'd wrangled a limousine for the night. So Meredith, Buddy Dial, Dan Reeves, Lee Roy Jordan, and I take off in this stretch Lincoln. Meredith is at the wheel.

I didn't know it at the time, but this was part of a tradition with the Cowboys. Sometime during the season on a road trip they would get each rookie drunk the night before a game. Rookies never played anyway so hangovers didn't mean a thing. There were only five rookies that year and tonight was my turn.

We get in the limo and Meredith turns around to me and says, "What do you want to drink tonight?"

"Oh, iced tea or something," I said.

"No," Meredith shot back, "I mean what do you want to *drink*?"

"Bourbon and seven?" I said.

"Okay. You drink a drink every time I drink and I'm paying for it," Meredith says.

When we got to the restaurant Meredith tells the waiter, "Bring him a Crown Royal Mist."

Well, a Crown Royal Mist is nothing but a whiskey snow cone. They take crushed ice and pour whiskey over it. It's worse than drinking straight out of the bottle because the ice takes away the bite so you can drink more.

I drink two or three and then I figured I better try to slow down this runaway train. Meredith is throwing down Scotch like it's lemonade, and there's no way I can keep up with him. So I pour my next drink in a potted plant. And damned if Meredith don't catch me. He just looked at me real mean and said, "Don't ever do that again."

I don't know what time we got in or how many of those whiskey slushes I had, but when I got up the next morning the last thing I wanted to do was play football. Finally I stumbled down to breakfast and Meredith looks like he just slept for 48 hours. He's bouncing around. He's singing and humming. He's laughing and telling jokes, and I'm just barely managing to keep my eggs down.

We played that afternoon and the whole goddamn game I don't get to play except on the suicide squads. It's the fourth quarter and Perkins is still out there. Meredith is still out there. What the hell is Landry thinking about? He's forgotten I'm there. It's a completely meaningless game and I'm still on the bench.

Meredith and Howard Cosell shown together during a promotion for ABC's Monday Night Football *in September 1971.* Photograph courtesy of Corbis.

Finally, with about two minutes left in the game, we get the ball and Landry looks around and says, "Hey, you, get in there." I don't think Landry knew my name the first three years I was with Dallas. It was always, "Hey, you!" So he points to me and I run on out there.

I get to the huddle and we're winning the game easy and Meredith looks over to me and says, "Hey, Walt, how's it going?"

He knows exactly how it's going. I'm all hungover and my head's killing me.

"Well," Meredith says, "I've been reading all your clippings. You were some hotshot in college. Let's see what you got."

He calls a "31 trap," which is right up the middle. The guard pulls, traps the nose tackle, and you go right over the center whether there's a hole there or not. And no matter how many yards you make, you're gonna take a beating.

Anyway, I carry the ball and make about a yard. And when I get back to the huddle Meredith says, "That ain't gonna do it. You were All-American. Let's try that again."

So he calls the same play right up the middle, and this time I make eight or nine yards and just barely get the first down. "Now that's better," he says. "Let's run it again."

Same goddamn play! And I ran that damn play nine straight downs until we ran the clock out. But along about the fourth play I snuck through a big hole in the line and two linebackers made a sandwich outta me. One hit me high and the other tore my leg off. I got up sorta slow but waved over to the sideline that I was okay. I wanted to play, so I limped back to the huddle and there's Meredith looking at me like I just tracked dog shit in on his new carpet.

"Let me tell you something," he says. "You ain't nothin' but a little pussy. You're hurtin'? Shit! You're nothin' but a little pussy, but I can't call you that in public so from now on I'm gonna call you 'Little Puddin.' But that means 'Little Pussy.' So every time I call you that you'll know what I'm talkin' about."

And the name stuck. Little Puddin. Damn! I always wanted a nickname like Rocky or Bone-crusher or Jackhammer. But Little Puddin was my name. I go back to a Cowboys reunion even today and guys still call me that. "Hey, Puddin, what's happening?" –W.G.

Cosell and MNF

Believe it or not, Don Meredith almost quit *Monday Night Football*. And Howard Cosell, of all people, made sure he didn't. But that still didn't keep Cosell from saying stupid things about Joe Don. Cosell said, "There was another, more complicated Meredith." Meredith was a put-on, he said. If anybody was a put-on, it was Cosell.

Cosell seemingly didn't know what he was talking about. He wrote a book: *I Never Played the Game.* He didn't have to tell me. It was obvious. I always said Cosell had the greatest recollection of unimportant facts of anybody alive. Who gives a crap who the 1938 Yankees' first, second, and third basemen were when you're watching the second half of a football game?

I never said Cosell wasn't smart, though. I met him once, at a restaurant in Buffalo, New York, and we visited for a while. I thought the guy was brilliant. And he's the one who really saved *Monday Night Football.*

A lot of people turned on *Monday Night Football* just to cuss Cosell. Bars had "I hate Cosell" contests. Whoever won got to throw a brick through the TV set. So a lot of people turned it on just to hear Meredith put Cosell down—the country boy putting down the city slicker. Anyway, Meredith was going to quit the show the first year it was on because he didn't think he was any good. But Cosell told him, "Don't quit. You're exactly what we need. You be the good guy and I'll be the bad guy and we'll both end up millionaires."

Dandy stuck it out, and just as Cosell predicted, the money came for them both. –W.G.

The Quarterback Shuttle

The 1961 season presented many problems for Tom Landry to ponder. The main problem was an overall lack of depth on the Cowboys' roster.

"We didn't have two of anything except quarterbacks," Landry said of the team that year, "so we had to alternate Eddie LeBaron and Don Meredith. If we had an extra guard or end, I probably would have used the same system as Paul Brown. But all we could spare was an extra quarterback."

And so in one of the more unorthodox moves ever made in the NFL, the quarterback shuttle was born and implemented in Dallas.

"I know all of the offense," Landry said of the QB shuttle system. "The quarterbacks don't have time, week to week, to assimilate it. Also, I have a lot more information available to me when I call a play. The quarterback coming off the field has to tell me about situations on the field, and he is in the best position of any player to tell me what the reaction of the defense is. I have the report from the coach in the press box, who has a good overall picture. And I've watched the play from the sideline with the other quarterback, checking to see if the defense is still keying the way we thought they would."

"Don didn't particularly like the shuttle," LeBaron said of the system, "but I didn't mind it. I thought it was working pretty well in 1962. We were leading the league in offense when I tore a muscle in my leg. We played the Giants, and if we'd have won we'd have been in pretty good shape. But on the first play of the game, I went up on my toes and popped a calf muscle. They couldn't stop us offensively that year, but we couldn't stop anyone defensively."

"I don't think we will always use this system," Meredith said at the time. "But it works now, and it has been a big help to me. Landry is a living IBM machine. He knows every defense in this league cold, and he never forgets anything. The time I spend on the sideline with him, analyzing the play I have just called and watching the development of the play Eddie is calling, is great experience."

In the end, it was Meredith who took over the full-time control of the team, eventually leading the Cowboys to the NFL Championship Game in 1966 and 1967.

Not Enough Work

Reflecting on his first star quarterback, Landry talked about his relationship with Meredith during an interview in 1990.

"Don and I just differed a little bit," Landry said. "I believe you have to pay a tremendous price to be a quarterback in this league, a tremendous price. You have to be very disciplined, you have to work and perform the way Roger [Staubach] did. So that was my problem with Don. He just didn't see it that way. Danny [White]? He loved the game, he really did...and he was very talented. Very talented. One of the toughest players I've ever coached. I'm talking about a guy who could get hurt and still play. I mean really hurt, cracked ribs, things like that."

Meredith probably played with more pain than any other quarterback of his time—maybe for all time. While that wasn't lost on Landry, who loved toughness in all his players, it wasn't quite enough.

"But we differed in the discipline I required in our system," Landry said. "Don didn't want that. I mean, he wanted a good time, lots of fun, but the guy played extremely well for me. He was a talented quarterback and I'm sorry he retired so soon. I really am."

Meredith retired in the summer of 1969 after nine years with the Cowboys.

chapter 5
From Next Year to Super

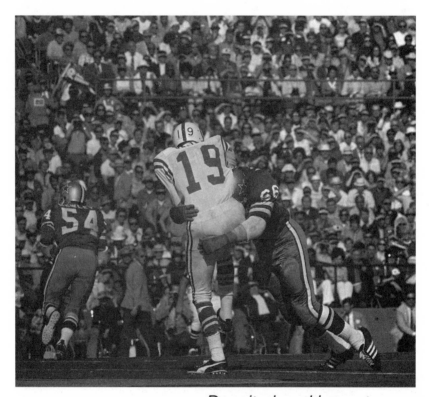

Despite knocking out Johnny Unitas, who left the game shortly after this hit by George Andrie in the first half, the Cowboys suffered a frustrating loss to the Colts in Super Bowl V.

To this day I can't understand how it was that we lost to the Baltimore Colts. We certainly gave it away. We made lots of mistakes.

—Lee Roy Jordan

The Monday Night Massacre

The Cardinals clobbered us in 1970, 38–0. And if that wasn't bad enough, the game was on *Monday Night Football*, the first time we played on Monday night. We played in the Cotton Bowl. It was one of those games; I mean, we knew we were better than the Cardinals, but every time we did something right, we did something wrong. It was either a fumble or an interception. It was one of those games where the harder you try, the worse it gets. Finally, toward the end of the game, if we hadn't been getting our ass kicked quite so bad, it would have been kind of laughable. But Coach Landry wasn't laughing, and unless he laughs, you can't laugh.

But we won the rest of our games. I think we were 5–4 at that point in the season or something like that. We didn't lose another game until the Super Bowl. –W.G.

Getting to the Big Game

We beat San Francisco in each of the NFC title games to get to the Super Bowl. And going into those games, there was doubt. If you think you're better than the other team and you think you're just going to run over them, you're probably fixin' to get your butt kicked. So I don't think at any point in the season, we said "Oh man, we're going to the Super Bowl." I know I didn't. I can't speak for everybody, but I know I never thought that. I never thought it until the plane ride home from San Francisco.

We were going to the Super Bowl.

I liked Miami, but I liked the food better in New Orleans, because I like oysters and stuff. But we may have had a better time in Miami, because like I said we were kinda overwhelmed at going to the Super Bowl, so we probably didn't take things as seriously as we did the next year. And the next year was pretty well strictly business. I mean, we went out to eat. Curfew was 11:00 PM. But we'd go out to eat or we'd walk down Bourbon Street. I never got drunk till after the game. I did get drunk the night of the game though. It was more of a business atmosphere than it was in Miami.

I think there was a difference in all of us. I think Coach Landry was a little bit relaxed at the first one because we'd never been, and his goal might have been just to get to the Super Bowl, too. And so maybe the next year he was a little more serious. I mean, I know we worked harder in practice the second year than the first. I mean it was more like a practice in Dallas, rather than at the Super Bowl, the second year. The first year we did a lot of stuff in sweats and didn't hit a lot. The next year we hit a little more. It seemed like just a regular practice, so I think he wanted us to think of it as a regular game, but at the same time that it was an important game and that the season wasn't complete yet because we hadn't won the Super Bowl. And to get the monkey off his back that Coach Landry couldn't win the big one. –W.G.

The Blunder Bowl

Super Bowl V was a nightmare for us. We played Baltimore, and before it was all over they called it the Blooper Bowl. There were five fumbles, six interceptions, and enough weird plays to last a season. And that was from the two teams that were supposed to be the best in football.

The outcome hinged on two strange and controversial plays. First Earl Morrall, Baltimore's old man quarterback, who came in when John Unitas was knocked out in the first quarter by George Andrie, threw a pass to Eddie Hinton. But Mel Renfro was all over Hinton. The ball went off Hinton and landed in the hands of Colt John Mackey, and Mackey walked into the end zone for an 80-yard score to tie the game. The only problem with that play is, it's illegal. A defensive man must touch the ball before another offensive player can catch a tipped pass. If you look at the films, the last person you can see touch the ball before Mackey was Hinton. But the officials ruled that Renfro had touched it. Mel swears to this day he never did.

In the third quarter we were leading 13–6 and had driven down to the 2-yard line. We were about to apply the knockout punch to the Colts. The handoff went to Duane [Thomas] and he fumbled the ball. No problem. Dave Manders recovered it.

But Billy Ray Smith of the Colts yelled, "Our ball! Our ball!" and he jumped up and down, really giving it the Oscar-nominee performance. And they bought it. Without even unpiling the players, they signaled that it was the Colts' ball. "It rolled right under me and I fell on it," Manders said. "I got up and handed the ball to the ref with a big smile on my face. I couldn't believe it when they gave it to Baltimore. I still can't believe it."

And that was that. If we score there, it makes it 20–6 and the game is over. But it wasn't.

The last disaster that day happened late in the game. Morton flipped a pass a little high out to Reeves, and he tipped the ball into the air, and the Colts' Mike Curtis intercepted it and ran it back to our 28. A couple plays later Jim O'Brien trotted out onto the field and kicked a field goal to beat us 16–13. –W.G.

Super Bowl VI

The first time a team goes to a Super Bowl they're just like a goose. They wake up in a new world every day. There's 9 million reporters and cameras and people shoving microphones in your face. That hype is powerful stuff. There are people around your hotel all the time and every one of them wants to be near you and give you whatever you want—and a lot of those people are pretty women.

You really can't handle it all the first time out. Your mind is on the people, the excitement, the chaos, the hoopla of the whole extravaganza. Everywhere except the game. Oh, you think you're concentrating on the game, but you're not really and you don't realize it until you come back a second time and remember how you acted, how you felt. The first time you play in a Super Bowl, the game is like a dream and you end up doing a lot of sleepwalking through it.

When we showed up in New Orleans we knew what to expect. We knew every reporter in the Western Hemisphere would be there. We knew we'd have to spend one to two hours a day in the press room. So it didn't bother us. We knew it was going to be a zoo. It wasn't unexpected anymore. It was expected. And that definitely helped us win.

The game was all business for us. There wasn't a lot of screaming and hollering in the locker room. We just took care of business.

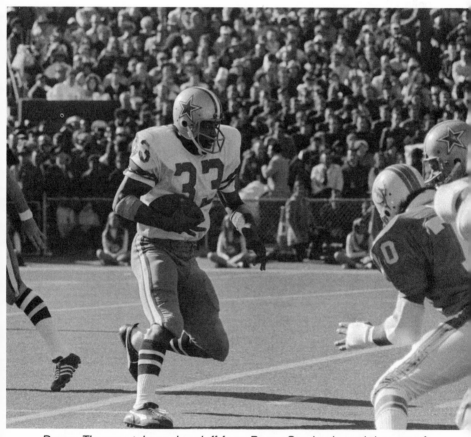

Duane Thomas, takes a handoff from Roger Staubach, and the rest of the Cowboys are focused on the task at hand in breaking through to win Super Bowl VI over the Miami Dolphins. Photograph courtesy of Corbis.

The Dolphins had a great young team that year. In fact, they went on to be one of the great teams of all time. In 1972 they posted a perfect season and went on to win two consecutive Super Bowls.

They had Jim Kiick and Larry Csonka and Bob Griese in the backfield, and their defense was a swarming, aggressive unit headed by Nick Buoniconti, Jake Scott, and Manny Fernandez. But they were still young in 1971, and our experience was too much for them.

Our game plan was to key on Buoniconti, because he controlled their defense. We started out giving the ball to me and running inside. If Nick floated outside on the play, I'd cut back. If he stayed in the middle, I'd go off the tight end. I just keyed on him. At halftime they adjusted to what we were doing, so then we faked the ball to me and pitched it to Duane and he ran wild outside.

That was probably the most perfect football game I've ever played in. We did nothing wrong. The defense stopped them cold, and the offense did whatever it wanted. We won 24–3 and it wasn't that close. With a minute to go Calvin Hill fumbled as he was crossing the goal line or it would have been 31–3. Roger was voted the Most Valuable Player.

The scene in the locker room after the victory was different than you'd expect. Nobody got stinking drunk and poured champagne all over everyone or threw Landry in the shower or tried to pants the TV guys. The feeling was one of relief. We'd finally done it. Oh, there was some hootin' and hollerin', but nobody went crazy.

We were a great team who'd had a great season and played like we were supposed to in the Super Bowl. Sitting in the locker room with a bottle of champagne, ripping tape off my arms, I looked over at Lilly and knew he was thinking what I was thinking: "Thank God, we've done it!"

They could say anything they wanted now. Except they couldn't say, "Dallas can't win the Big One." –W.G.

"What If?"

"To be honest, I really hated when we lost that Super Bowl," the Cowboys' Pettis Norman said of the loss to the Colts in Super Bowl V. "I know we should have won the game. We should have won that game without any hesitation. I just didn't brood over it as much as I did the two Green Bay games in '66 and '67. And maybe it was the false surroundings, the constant distractions leading up to it. You hardly had a chance to focus on the game.

"One of the interesting things to speculate about is, what if we had won that game? One scenario is that Craig [Morton] stays and Roger [Staubach] leaves. How can you replace a guy who wins a Super Bowl? With anybody, even if he messes up the first half of the season, how would you justify replacing that guy?

"And who knows where the Cowboys would have gone had that happened. Would they have won two or three more Super Bowls during that decade? It's wild when you think about it. That one game was *the* pivotal game in Cowboys history."

Crushing the Orange

After losing to the Steelers in Super Bowl X, the Cowboys were anxious to reclaim the NFL championship when they met the Denver Broncos in Super Bowl XII.

"I was extra hungry facing the Denver Broncos in Super Bowl XII," the Cowboys' Harvey Martin said in *Super Bowl Sunday*. "Super Bowl X was like the circus for us, because we were so happy to be there. That was my third year in the NFL, Ed 'Too Tall' Jones's second. We were just babies. We were like, 'Oh my God, we're in the Super Bowl. I can't believe it.' During the game we met a great Steeler football team. In XII we didn't have time to get caught up in the hoopla. We were there for business. We wanted to be world champions. And that helped us so much because we had been there, done that. We were no longer the starry-eyed kid in the Super Bowl. We were there to win.

Ed "Too Tall" Jones crushes Denver Broncos quarterback Craig Morton during the Cowboys' 27–10 win in Super Bowl XII in New Orleans on January 15, 1978.

"A lot of that mentality was from the core group of guys that lost and didn't want to lose again. They wanted to go out and play ball. They were willing to pay the price to become the best. We all cried together after that loss to the Steelers, so against Denver we said, 'Let's go out and play football.' A lot of guys wanted the perks that went with being a Dallas Cowboy and being an NFL champion, but the only way you can get those perks is to win. The main thing we talked about all week leading up to the Denver game was that if you want all the adulation that goes with being No. 1, then you have to become No. 1.

"The first thing I remember about walking onto the field in the Louisiana Superdome for the first time was seeing Denver's

Tom Landry is carried off the field by his team including Larry Cole (63) and Butch Johnson (86) after the Cowboys beat the Broncos in Super Bowl XII.

'Orange Crush' come out and all the people wearing that ugly orange. They figured the Broncos had a chance to win. (We didn't think they did.) The second thing that comes to mind was the concentration, the focus, on our side.

"We had an excellent defense on those teams back in the 1970s. In fact, we ended the Super Bowl XII season as the number one defense in the NFL. And we actually had the number one offense in the NFL. Our defense was hungry. We were a bunch of opportunistic guys. We had fought our way through one glorious season in the 1970s, when it was tough, playing ball in the '70s. Today there are good football teams, but there is free agency. In the 1970s, guys stayed with one team for the duration of their careers. It wasn't an easy chore for us to go through that season like we did. When we went on the football field, we could not let up until we finished that one game.

"The one thing that got me the most was at the end of the game, when Randy White and I were standing next to each other, neither one of us having a clue we would be MVPs. We were just happy as hell we were winning the ballgame. I'll never forget when CBS announcer Pat Summerall came out and said, 'Folks, for the first time in history there are two Most Valuable Players.' Even at that moment, it was still totally far away from my mind. Then Summerall continued, 'Harvey Martin and Randy White.' I just lost it. I was not ready for that announcement. I was not ready for that at all."

.

chapter 6
Roger the Dodger

Roger Staubach, who played quarterback at Navy, poses with the Heisman Trophy he won in New York on December 11, 1963.

He (Roger Staubach) was the greatest hero of his time.... He was the hero of a nation, not just the Cowboys or even the league.

—Tex Schramm

When Staubach Joined the Team

When Roger Staubach joined the Cowboys in 1969 as a 27-year-old rookie, nobody figured he'd do much of anything. Yeah, he'd been the Heisman Trophy winner at the Naval Academy. But that was way back in 1963. The Cowboys had drafted him in the 10th round of the 1964 draft on a longshot that in five years, when Roger's tour of duty was up, he'd be both willing and able to play in the NFL.

But Roger Staubach, of course, was a different kind of person than your normal *Homo sapiens.* He'd be out on a destroyer in the Gulf of Tonkin or some ungodly place for nine months at a time, and then he'd take his leave and come to training camp and work out! That's how sick he was. We'd see him out there sweating his ass off through two-a-days and we'd say, "What in the hell is he doin' here? He can't even play for three, four more years."

The guy had been off serving his country for 11 months and he gets three weeks off and he's out there every day working his butt off. Training camp is exactly like going to boot camp all over again. In fact, I've been to both boot camp and training camp, and I'd rather go to boot camp. But Roger'd be out there with us every year. Now you've got to admire that kind of dedication. The principles Roger stood for, he wouldn't waver from. If a guy won't compromise his beliefs, no matter what they are, you gotta respect him.

Roger is not a hypocrite. He don't say, "Hey, you oughta do this." And then he does something else. Roger just says, "This is what I do." He don't try to tell you what you oughta do. He ain't a bit phony.

One thing about Roger Staubach, I've always respected him. I always will. I don't want to spend a lot of time with him, but I sure do respect his ass.

See, Roger just wasn't given to having a good time. He's against having fun. It's in his genes or something. Anything that's fun, you're not supposed to do. That's the way he feels.

One time somebody said, "Boy, wouldn't you love to have your kid grow up to be more like Roger Staubach?" And Meredith said, "No way. I'd want my kid to have more fun."

That's the way I feel about Roger. I could never figure out why he couldn't loosen up and have more fun.

My wife and I had a party up at our place one year, and we invited a bunch of the Cowboys, and I called Roger and he said, "Oh, yeah, we'll be there." Then he called back about a day before the party and said he had to go away on business.

Next year, same deal. I invited everybody and Roger calls again the day before the party and says, "Oh, Walt, I'm sorry. I'll be out of town."

"Roger," I said, "nobody gives a shit if you come. You're not the life of the goddamn party anyway. I'll bet tomorrow night not one sonuvabitch at that party will come up to me and say, 'I wonder where Roger is. It just ain't the same without him.' So don't feel bad about it, Roger." –W.G.

Captain America

Roger Staubach was the epitome of what Landry thought a quarterback should be. He was the most dedicated guy you'll ever be around. If somebody did a hundred sit-ups, Roger was going to do a hundred and one. If somebody ran a mile in six minutes, Roger would do it in 5:59. If somebody threw the ball 60 yards, he was going to throw it 61.

Landry felt that when you've got a guy as dedicated as Roger was, it was very easy to get the other players to go that extra mile to win. Because your leader was out there doing it. Besides that, Roger was a good Christian, went in and served his country, and had a great wife and kids.

Landry thought he'd died and gone to heaven.

There was only one problem; we already had a great quarterback in Craig Morton. And he wasn't gonna just sit back and let this anchor-cranking bastard take his place.

Morton had tremendous physical talents and a great football mind. He could throw the football 70 yards flat-footed, and he could read defenses like you read a book. And Craig would play with pain.

But Craig Morton, like Don Meredith before him, was a party animal. In fact, he was the whole zoo. Meredith was not the kind of guy who would give you the impression that football was the most important thing in his life. He wasn't going to push himself to work hard to be the best. He let his natural talents do his work for him, and if that wasn't going to be enough, to hell with it. To Meredith football and life were separate. And he sure wasn't going to let football interfere with his pursuit of all that the world had to offer in the way of life, libation, and the pursuit of women.

Morton was like Meredith. Football was not his whole life. He was more dedicated than Meredith, but that wasn't saying a lot.

Craig was famous for his partying. That boy could rock 'n' roll, let me tell you. He spent money like it was fertilizer and he had a couple thousand head of cattle. And, boy, he had some good-lookin' girlfriends. I don't know any of their names, but he'd come to a party and he always had somebody shiny with him. But, hell, he didn't have a wife or family and he was the quarterback for the Dallas Cowboys, which was glamorous as hell, and he had a big contract, so why not enjoy it?

Morton proved he was a great athlete. You'd have to be great to stay out as many nights as he did and do all the crazy stuff he did and still make practice. The guy was phenomenal.

Now Staubach? Well, two beers was a decadent evening for Roger.

Roger and Craig were opposites on the field, too. Morton was your basic pocket passer. He was gonna stay in the pocket and deliver the football regardless of what kind of pass rush they threw at him. Not Roger. At the first sign of pressure, he was gone. He created havoc for defenses with his scrambling ability. Roger the Dodger.

They were both great in their own way. So right away we had a quarterback controversy. The press, the fans, the players—hell,

Captain Comeback peers downfield for a receiver as he prepares to pass against Pittsburgh in the first half of Super Bowl X.

even Landry couldn't figure out who to play. At the time, Roger hadn't made the Hall of Fame yet. He hadn't led us to five Super Bowls. He was just a rookie yet to pass the test. And he was pushing an All-Pro quarterback. You think Landry had a few things to think about? Even the team was split. The defense liked Roger because he made things happen. But the offensive guys loved Craig. We thought he was a better quarterback. He knew the offense better than Roger. He could read defenses better. He had a better feel for the game and a better arm. And Roger hadn't played professional football for very long, whereas Morton had been playing for six or seven years.

Morton was more regimented in the Landry system. When Staubach first came up, if things didn't go his way he scrambled. He ran everywhere. And Landry didn't like that. And neither did the offense. The offense had confidence that it could score with Landry's system and the players it had. When Staubach took off on one of his runs, it was Roger against the world. Throw out Dallas's multiple offense; throw out Speed Inc.; throw out Bob Hayes, the fastest man in the world; throw out the best blocking line in the business. Yeah, and throw out "I'll getcha four yards" Garrison. It was Roger Staubach versus the NFL.

In the end Landry went with Staubach. But even then he had to use them both. Morton took us to the Super Bowl in 1970 against Baltimore. Then, in 1971, he lost out to Roger in the great quarterback debate. But Roger got injured midway through the next season, and Craig took over and led us to the division title again. Roger stepped in during the playoffs that year and regained his starting position, but Morton was the one who got us there. –W.G.

Learning

Roger scrambled a lot when he first started playing because he didn't read defenses that well. But as he got better and more acclimated to what the hell was going on—the way to read defenses and stuff—he didn't scramble as much. Roger had a great knack of knowing where people were on the field, the defensive guys. When you watch all the films and the way he spun away from people and possible tackles, it was just a cinch, almost a fact, that he could see 'em. He just knew they were coming, and he knew where they were coming from.

It seemed from the very beginning that Roger had an uncanny knack to get away from people and make big plays out of busted plays. But as far as when Roger came into the league, he was like all rookies—a new guy. And all new guys, regardless of how good they are, still need a while to get acclimated to the league and higher level of play. It takes a while to read defenses and know where to go. And Roger didn't know this stuff. How could he? But he learned, just like all of us who come into the league. You think you know, but you really don't, and the only way you learn is to play. Roger got better the more he played.   –W.G.

The Plays

Roger would change the plays some, but whether Landry was upset depended on whether it worked or not. Sometimes Roger would say, "Oh, I didn't hear that" when they'd send in the play or send signals or when we used to rotate tight ends and guards and everything before they had the headsets. Or Roger would say, "Hey, that won't work. Against this defense that just won't work." So he would change the play, and sometimes it worked and sometimes it didn't. And I'm sure when it didn't Coach Landry would have a few kind words to say to Roger. But Roger was a thinking quarterback. He studied and he knew a lot. He didn't too much the first couple of years he played—nobody does. After that, he knew what was going on.

I don't think any one person has ever won any team game. But did Roger have a part in us winning the Super Bowl? Absolutely. Did Lance Alworth, who was probably the greatest receiver I ever played with, have a part of it? Yes. Did Mike Ditka have a part of it?

Roger played great throughout his career, but he had bad games, too. It wasn't like he played great every week of every season. Nobody can do that. Look at Peyton Manning. Dallas beat them this year (2006) when he wasn't on. Some days you're just not 100 percent. –W.G.

Getting a Shot

"Against Baltimore, all we had to do was have a halfway good passing game," Staubach said of the loss to the Colts in Super Bowl V. "And after that game, that was the lowest I ever felt. Because before that, Landry had said to me, 'It takes four years to become a starting quarterback.' Plus I wasn't young anymore. I didn't know where I was going. If I couldn't play in a game and really help the team with Craig injured, what was I going to do when the guy was healthy?

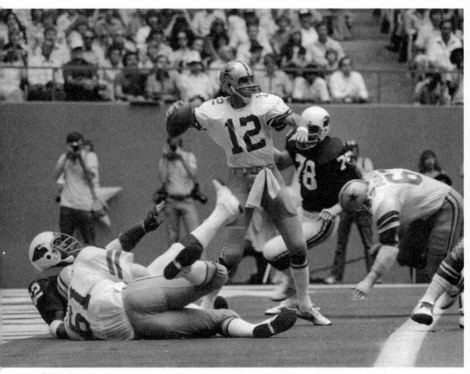

Staubach was always cool under pressure, as he demonstrates here by hanging tough in the pocket against the St. Louis Cardinals in an October 1979 game.

"After the game I felt that was possibly going to be it for me in Dallas. We were flying back to Dallas, and Tom Landry came back and sat with me for a few minutes. I was sitting with my wife, and he said, 'You will get your opportunity to be a starting quarterback this coming season.' And when he said that, I was rejuvenated, and I had a great off-season, worked hard, and in '71 Craig came back in great shape, and we competed for the job."

Cowboys and Indians

In good years and bad, the Cowboys' games with the Washington Redskins are always heated and bitter.

"We had a big rivalry against the Redskins," Staubach said. "Diron Talbert was a big defensive tackle, and Chris Hanburger was a linebacker, and Kenny Houston was a safety. So, it was like a playoff game every time we played the Redskins. Defensively, we got to know them very well. I think my favorite [Redskins game] was in 1971 when we were 4–3 in the middle of the year and the Redskins were really on a roll. It was the first year they had the 'Over the Hill Gang,' with George Allen. We lost to them in Dallas and we went up to Washington and beat them. It was part of a 10-game winning streak we had, and that was the key game. And then my last year we beat them 35–34 in a comeback to win the division. So, those two games were the most memorable."

The Best Quarterback

While there isn't a consensus on who the greatest Cowboys quarterback is, Staubach would get a fair share of the votes.

"I think a case could be made for Meredith if [he] had played on a better football team and not been killed," Bob Lilly said. "But Roger, as far as the ones I've played with, he came at a time when he had a better football team and he also brought a great deal of leadership to our team, which we really needed. And he was very disciplined, and had his naval training as well as his fierce competitive spirit. The other thing about Roger, he was totally healthy—he didn't have any knee problems like Craig Morton did. He didn't have any injuries that would set him back. He was also very cordial to all the players on our team. He hung out with all the guys, he was just a regular guy, and just a real, real pleasure to be around.

"His leadership skills were an immense support for our team to get us up on top, because we were right at the top for a long time and never could get up on the hill. And I think that was a big thing. The other was that he had a great sixth sense about football and, like all great quarterbacks, he could feel the pressure coming from behind without ever seeing anybody, and was able to scramble and to get out of the pocket and make a nice throw downfield.

He won many, many ballgames—I think 26—in the last few seconds of the game. So, I'd say Roger."

Tom Landry on Staubach

"Roger Staubach especially wanted to play," Landry said in a 1990 interview. "In one of our quarterback meetings, I talked about the importance of experience, pointing out that there wasn't a quarterback in the league who's ever won a championship with less than three years of experience. Even Joe Namath was in his fourth year before he won the Super Bowl.

"At that Roger exploded. 'How can you judge every individual by the same yardstick? If you do that, I don't have a chance to start because I'm only in my second year. You've got to judge everyone separately!'

"A little taken aback by his outburst, I said, 'Roger, see me after the meeting.' Then after everyone else left, I tried to explain my feelings about developing quarterbacks: how the mental knowledge of the game is so crucial in the pros. How I felt so many quarterbacks had been ruined and lost the confidence so essential to a good quarterback because they were sent in before they had the understanding needed to succeed against NFL defenses.

"Roger wasn't convinced. 'Coach,' he said, 'I feel I can physically make up for any mental shortcomings.'

"I wished Roger could be more patient, I had no doubts the necessary knowledge was going to come in time. He was not only intelligent, but one of the most dedicated athletes I've ever known. If he gave his all, he knew he could succeed."

The Dropped Pass

It is one of the most famous incomplete passes in the Cowboys' illustrious history: Jackie Smith's dropped pass in Super Bowl XIII while wide open in the end zone.

"I feel badly, of course," Smith said of the dropped pass. "If I had caught it, I think we would have at least tied them [the Steelers]. It was a great call. I just missed it. I slipped a little but still should have had it. I've dropped passes before, but not any with that much importance.

"Maybe I would have caught it with my hands, but in that situation you are trying to be sure so you want to use your chest. Then I lost my footing, my feet ended up in front of me and I think the ball went off my hip. It's hard to remember—those things happen so quickly."

"When I started to throw it there was no question in my mind," Staubach said. "I knew it would be completed. But I took too much off. It wasn't a good throw. If you're casting blame, it's 50 percent my fault and 50 percent Jackie's. I know this: it wasn't for lack of experience, because we're the two oldest guys on the team."

The Cowboys made a valiant comeback late in the game but lost to the Steelers, 35–31.

chapter 7
Cowboy Characters

Duane Thomas, shown here breaking away from Jets linebacker John Ebersole in a December 1971 game, could have run for a lot more yards for the Cowboys had he made better decisions.

Hollywood was sort of an alter ego of drug addiction and women. Hollywood never played football. He was hanging out with Marvin Gaye and doing wild things.

—Thomas "Hollywood" Henderson

The Mysterious Duane Thomas

Duane Thomas was pro football's Jekyll and Hyde. He played for Dallas for two years and in that time established himself as the premier running back in football. Duane also established himself as the premier pain in the ass.

Now, Duane was an outstanding talent, that was for sure. He was a hell of a running back, filled with natural ability. He could run with power and speed. He was smooth as silk when he ran, and he had moves that had linebackers grabbing for air. He'd just lope along and suddenly he'd be through a hole and gone.

I believe Duane was a genuinely nice person. In his rookie year you couldn't have asked for a more cooperative, soft-spoken guy. He worked hard, and he was nice as hell to everybody.

In his second year he wouldn't talk to anyone. He just stalked around brooding. Bob Hayes nicknamed him "Othello."

I honestly don't think anyone knows why he didn't talk. I don't think even Duane knew. He probably got some bad advice. But whatever it was, he just wouldn't talk to any body—I mean nobody. Not just the press or the fans. He wouldn't talk to anybody on the team, either. Not the coaches, not the players, not the other running backs. Nobody.

When they took roll call at team meetings, he wouldn't answer when his name was called. When Tom asked him why, Duane said, "You can see me. I'm sitting right there."

Thomas hurt himself in a game once, and Jethro Pugh came over and asked him, "How's the knee?" Duane said, "Why you wanna know? You a doctor?"

Hey, he was a horse's ass.

People always asked me, "How did you and Duane get along?" Well, I liked Duane. I always liked him. I liked him when he was weird. I didn't give a damn if he ever talked, because he played. That son of a bitch played. And I don't say that even about a lot of guys who did talk.

One time Duane scored a touchdown against San Francisco in a playoff game in Texas Stadium. They called an audible at the goal line, and Duane went to the wrong side of the formation. I told him, "Duane, other side." He moved over. They pitched out to him and he scored.

A writer asked me after the game, "Did you line up in the wrong spot?" And I said, "Yes."

They found out later that I lied to them and they came back. "Why didn't you tell us Thomas was lined up in the wrong spot?"

"Because y'all been on his ass all year."

The bottom line, I liked the guy.

Actually, Duane and I did talk. We played in the same backfield, so we had to talk because backs got to talk. You can't play in the same backfield unless you do. You'd be running all over each other. So there's a lot of talk that goes on between backs when they break the huddle, set up, and when they call audibles or when the defenses change alignments. If you don't talk, it don't work.

Of course I never talked to him before or after the game. But during the game we talked plenty.

I never had any real problem with Duane except in practice. He'd stand off by himself during practice. And sometimes he'd practice and sometimes he wouldn't. Oh, Duane would run with the first-team offense. But then when it came time for the defense to practice, he'd refuse to run. We'd all run on the dummy teams to simulate the opponent's offense. If you had three backs, you'd run every third play. But Duane wouldn't do it, which put an extra load on me and the other running backs. And that pissed us off.

I got my ass chewed out in practice one day because it was Duane's turn to run a dummy play and he was off dicking around as usual. "What the hell's wrong with Thomas?" I yelled.

Landry jumped all over me, (and) then he said, "It's your turn to run. Get in there." Oh, that went over big with the rest of the veterans.

The worst part of it was that Landry let him get away with it. Anybody else would have gotten the boot. You don't want to practice? Good-bye. But not Duane Thomas. Landry left him alone. So while the rest of us kicked butt during practice, Duane stood over on the sidelines chewing gum. And Landry didn't say shit.

I'm not sure of Landry's motivation. He knew Duane had some kind of problem. He didn't know what it was, but Tom's the kind of guy who cares about people. There's no telling how many hours and days and weeks and months Tom spent on Duane, trying to straighten him out. And I think Landry looked at Duane as his one big failure. He wanted to get Duane back on the right track. Tom wanted to save him, wanted to give him a chance to get back to being a human being again.

But it didn't work.

That's when Landry really lost the respect of the veteran players. Because all of a sudden we now had a double standard. Landry had never had one set of rules for one guy and another set for everybody else. You performed, you fit in, you went by the rules, or you were gone, baby. Guys like Bob Lilly and Lee Roy Jordan and Chuck Howley—every one of them had been All-Pro for years, and Landry never so much as let them take an extra piss during practice.

Ironically, Landry's failure with Duane showed the strength of his character. It showed how much he really did care about his players. Most other coaches would have gotten rid of Thomas right away if he'd given them that kind of trouble. And, in fact, they did. After he left Dallas, Thomas was traded to team after team, even though everybody knew he was one of the best backs in football.

If Landry was truly like his image—cold, calculating, humorless, and unemotional—he would have cut Thomas without a second thought. Duane ran us right into the Super Bowl that year, and it just about destroyed the team. A Super Bowl is supposed to bring everybody together, and here we were holding up the Super Bowl trophy and everybody was pissed off.

In the end I thought the whole thing was sad. When I look back at football, what I miss the most is the other players. The closeness that you develop with 40 guys over a nine-year period of time. It's a team sport, so you better like other people.

Duane Thomas was at odds with his teammates. And here was one of the greatest pure talents ever to come along, and he had two good years then bounced from team to team for three, four years not doing much of anything.

And then he was gone. –W.G.

Misquoted

Bob Belden was a third-string quarterback with the Cowboys in 1969–70. Bob St. John, a writer with the *Dallas Morning News*, asked me about him.

"What do you think Bob Belden feels like after running the scout team and sometimes he travels with the team and sometimes he doesn't?"

"He probably feels like a bastard at a family reunion," I said. I didn't think that was a bad quote, and was trying to be funny. The next day, St. John comes running up to me. "Walt, I've gotta apologize." And I said, "Why?" And he said, "Well, I turned in the story I wrote on you and I didn't want to put bastard in there, so instead I wrote that Belden feels like a black sheep at a family reunion. But when they set the type, they left out 'sheep.'"

So it came out that Walt Garrison said that Bob Belden feels like he's a black at a family reunion.

I got a couple of letters from some black folks. But Frank Clarke, a receiver for us, rammed the paper at me and said, "Did you say that?" And I said, "You know I didn't." And he said, " I know you didn't." And that was it. He turned around and walked off and that was it.

And so people, the guys that knew me, knew it wasn't something that I would have said. I mean I jacked with the black guys and I jacked with the white guys. Black and white has nothing to do with it. But I got some hate mail. The NAACP might have written something to me. Afterward, I told St. John, "Let me tell you something *buddy*: from now on if I say shit, you write it; or bastard, you write it; or son-of-a-bitch, you write that. *Don't change my words.* But don't try to make something up. If you can't print what I say, then don't print any of it."

Bob and I had a good relationship from then on. –W.G.

A Role Model

They say it's what happens between the white lines, even though you're snortin' up some white lines. Lawrence Taylor, he definitely belongs in the Hall of Fame. They say if they go with what happens on the field, but I think everything goes into being a football player. You're a role model whether you want to be or not. Players say "I don't want to be a role model." Well then don't play football, because you are one. And that's why you got high school kids and junior high kids and everybody doing these little dances in the end zone and all this crap that's got nothing to do with football other than to bring attention to one person. As far as I'm concerned it's still a team game, and if all 11 of you want to jump up and down and do all that shit, that's more than fine. But if one guy gets off by hisself and brings attention like T.O. [Terrell Owens] does or like Emmitt [Smith] used to before they put the Emmitt rule in, where you couldn't take your helmet off, that's just stupid. –W.G.

Iron Mike Joins the Cowboys

I was happy as hell when Mike Ditka joined the Cowboys in 1969—he was a tough sonuvabitch. Ditka was the kind of guy if there was a brick wall in front of him and he could walk just 10 feet down and go around it, he'd say, "F*ck it!" and try and run right through it.

Ditka was mean. He walked into a restaurant one night, walked over to a table with some chairs stacked on it and just raked them all off with his big ol' forearm and motioned for us to come on over and sit down.

Nobody said a word. I know why too. Ditka had the foulest temper of any man I've ever met. It was so bad people used to like to get him mad just to see what he'd do because he could lose control in a slim second and anything could happen. That was the fun of it—the element of surprise.

I used to go golfing with Ditka and [Dan] Reeves and Dave Edwards. Mike threw his club after about every shot. He used to throw stuff all over. Hell, I'd just started playing golf and I thought it was part of the game. Get mad, throw a club, cuss, beat your club on the ground, break the damn thing, throw it in the lake. I thought that's how you played golf. Ditka would throw a club over in the woods and I'd go on over there and get it and put it in my bag. That's how I got my first set of clubs. –W.G.

A Remarkable Player

Thomas "Hollywood" Henderson came to the Cowboys from tiny Langston University in Oklahoma. A first-round pick in the 1975 draft, Henderson had athletic prowess that quickly earned him playing time. By the 1977 season, the outside linebacker had earned All-Pro honors. He was such an outstanding football player that the Cowboys used him to run reverses on kickoffs from time to time, with him scoring on one occasion. He was one of the first linebackers to run a 4.6 in the 40-yard dash.

As athletically gifted as he was, he was also a fast runner in the world of drugs, alcohol, and fast women.

"Oh, Thomas Henderson was a remarkable player," Landry said of his star linebacker, but he still questioned whether or not Dallas should have drafted him. "I remember, we sent our scout over to his school in Oklahoma, and he showed up just to watch him practice, but when he got there they were scrimmaging but Thomas wasn't. He was in his clothes, wasn't in a uniform. But he came over to the scout—he knew who he was—and asked him, 'Hey, do you want to see me scrimmage?' And the scout, I can't remember who it was, said, 'Hey, sure, that's why we came over here, hoping you'd scrimmage.' So Thomas says, 'Okay, wait a minute,' and he runs away, puts on his uniform, runs back out onto the field, checks himself into the scrimmage, makes two or three flashy tackles, and then walks over to our scout and says, 'Okay, have you seen enough?'"

And he had. So Henderson ended the audition and put his street clothes back on.

"That should have told me right then that he was trouble, because, you know, he wasn't a disciplined football player," Landry said. "But I didn't really break the mold with Thomas. He was a great, great athlete, a remarkable player; and until he got himself all messed up, he was okay. Oh, sure, he talked a lot, and he was loud, and he got on people's nerves, but he was kind of nice about it, a good kid, and he was such a great player, such a showman."

The worst part for Landry was not being able to read Henderson.

"I couldn't tell whether or not he was serious," Landry said. "He was another great talent wasted. The most disappointing thing is, I just couldn't help them enough. I feel guilty that I couldn't get them back on the right track. Once you get on coke or crack, you're destined for trouble. Nobody is going to change you, either."

Doubting Thomas

"My disappointment in the case of Duane Thomas is I had no idea what he was doing," Landry said of the Cowboys' problematic running back. "At the end of the '60s, the drug culture came in, and everybody wanted to do their own thing. I knew something was different with Duane, but I didn't know what it was. Boy, it's a shame to see a guy's career being ruined.

"My feeling is, if Duane Thomas continued to play the way he did the couple of years he was in there, it would have been very hard for Pittsburgh to beat us [in the Super Bowl]. If we had Duane and Calvin Hill, together they would have made an impact."

Dallas Goes Hollywood

Thomas Henderson played the type of football Landry mandated, but the linebacker didn't like it.

"I disliked Landry's football system, because it is for disciplined players, and I was not a disciplined player," Henderson said in *Cowboys Have Always Been My Heroes*. "Whenever there was a concept that I saw that had restraint and that limited my ability to play the position, I balked at it, wouldn't do it.

"Let me tell you what I would do. I *never* scored more than a 60 percent in his game film evaluations after any one game. See, every week Landry graded his football players on who did the right steps, and who had the right angle on your drop, and were you in position and did you read the play right? I never scored very high, but I finally found a way to appease Landry. I would take the initial steps toward what he wanted me to do, and then I would take off to pursue the angle I wanted to pursue. And I made All-Pro. So there was a way to play Landry's deal and get away.

"I always did it that way. They just didn't like to see me doing it. See, intuitively I picked it up, but see, football to me was the snap of the ball, and then the concert of the dance. In other words, I saw the game real quick at the snap of the ball. I couldn't see the game on computer printouts or little round circles and arrows pointing here and there. You could show me a play, but you couldn't show me how to defend it. Because in football, everybody is not always where they are supposed to be, and in football, for me, it's up to me to make the tackle. It's not up to me to depend on inside pursuit or 'This guy is coming and so you contain it.' No. My deal was, 'I gotta make the play. If I don't make the play, nobody is.' And Landry's system was to play in concert, and so I never played like that. As a matter of fact, Landry paid me the highest

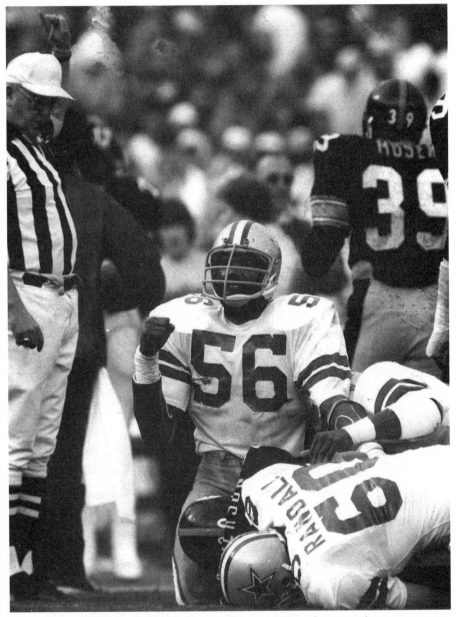

*Thomas "Hollywood" Henderson pumps his fist after stopping
Pittsburgh Steelers back Larry Anderson during the second quarter of
Super Bowl XIII in Miami on January 21, 1979.*

compliment. It took him four years. He called me a pro. Because he finally saw that I had taken the good from his system and used it to my advantage.

"By my last season with the Cowboys, I contend that I was the hardest working man in the franchise. I was playing defense, third-down defense, kickoffs, kickoff returns, punts, punt returns, field goal rush, field goal block. I was playing *everywhere* except offense. I remember Gil Brandt said to me one time after I asked him for a $250,000 salary, 'We don't even pay Roger Staubach $250,000.' I said, 'He doesn't work as much as I do.'

"There was one thing I liked about Landry. He taught me something. He said, 'When you keep your shoulders parallel to the line of scrimmage, you're the most powerful thing on the field.' So my little skinny 215-pound ass had to have every possible trick, and that was one of the great ones. And I used to knock 300-pound tackles and guards on their asses by squaring up to the line of scrimmage and just knocking the shit out of them.

"That was the thing he taught me that helped me. As a matter of fact, Landry would come out sometimes and try to give me instructions on how to play linebacker, and I'd say, 'But you never played linebacker, did you? I know how to do this. Why don't you go and talk to those defensive backs.' And the team would just die laughing.

"The other guys, particularly the older guys, were afraid of Landry. Jethro Pugh, Rayfield Wright, Mel Renfro, some of the older black gentlemen on the Cowboys had experienced racism from a powerless point of view. And that doesn't mean that they weren't great men. But when they saw me being free and expressive, they would get all upset. I would even smoke cigarettes in my locker. Shit, those guys would go smoke in their car.

"I fired up in my locker. Why shouldn't I smoke? I was 22 years old. There was no rule. But the older guys wouldn't do it. I did. I smoked on the airplane, everywhere. I took smoke breaks.

"When I first became a Dallas Cowboy, Landry was this dictator, this Castro, this Khrushchev, this Saddam Hussein, this

Ayatollah. You know. You didn't talk back. It was religious. It was communism. It was all these things you fear, and people marched around like they were in the Red Army. And I was walking around going, 'What the f*ck are you all doing around here? Lighten the f*ck up. F*ck him. He's just a f*cking coach.'

"It never occurred to me to be afraid of Landry. It never occurred to me to take him as seriously as he thought he was."

chapter 8
America's Team

George Teague carries an American flag and joins his team on the playing field at Texas Stadium on September 23, 2001, before kickoff with the San Diego Chargers.

By 1978 we could tell how much the
Cowboys had become a part of America's
culture. Our popularity was at an
all-time peak, and it wasn't just in Dallas.
It was on a national basis.

—Drew Pearson

America's Team—what a stupid nickname.
That's just ignorant as heck.
I mean that's stupid.

—Walt Garrison

America's Team

I suppose it might have been inevitable, but maybe not. Anyway, some wise guy at NFL Films decided to make up a name for the Cowboys, "America's Team," and boy, it went over like a lead balloon in every town in America except Dallas.

But maybe we were America's Team. Dallas had the number one TV ratings in pro football, and we seemed to be on the tube every week. We had Dandy Don, the playboy quarterback, and Bullet Bob Hayes, the fastest human on earth. We had a high-powered offense that led the league in scoring, and a high-tech stadium. And we won a lot. Plus, we had the best-looking cheerleaders.

But all that name ever brought us was grief. Everybody was out to get us. You'd go into a town and there'd be R-rated signs all over about America's Team. The Oilers beat us one year, and after the game Bum Phillips, the Oilers coach, said, "Well, they might be America's team, but the Oilers are Texas's team." The problem was, Dallas was the most glamorous team in the league. We were showered with publicity and endorsements.

Still, I think it's a stupid name. –W.G.

The Cheerleaders

They used to have high school cheerleaders at the Cotton Bowl. A different high school would send their cheerleading squad down and they'd get over there on the sidelines and cheer. And then Tex Schramm came up with the idea for the cheerleaders. He'd probably been to one or two too many titty bars and thought it was a good idea.

And it was a good idea.

Tex came up with a lot of unique ideas that hadn't been done before. I never really noticed the cheerleaders, to be honest. People would ask me if I watched the cheerleaders. I'd say, "I'm kind of busy on Sunday." You really didn't sit there and look at the

The Dallas Cowboys Cheerleaders take their places on the field at Texas Stadium prior to the cowboys game with the St. Louis Rams in January 2006.

cheerleaders. And they had, like, four groups, one at each end zone or one at the other end.

I never actually met a cheerleader until after I'd retired. And that one used to go to Lewisville High School, as a matter of fact. There was some kind of grand opening at some store, and they had four of the Dallas Cowboys cheerleaders there, and this one came over to me and introduced herself. And of all things, I knew her ma.

The thing was, you couldn't date them. So that kind of stopped any interest the players might have had right there. I don't actually know that anybody I remember ever talked about the cheerleaders. The only time you ever saw them was on Sunday, and you didn't really see them then. So like I said, I guess some of the guys who weren't playing might have seen them, but I never did notice them. –W.G.

The Name Is Born

A remarkable thing happened to the Cowboys before the 1979 season began. For no reason other than lack of a decent movie title, they were dubbed with a nickname that would make sure they were hated everywhere except in Dallas.

When the team gathered for a private viewing of the previous season's highlight film from NFL Films, no one was prepared for what they were about to see.

"Everybody started laughing," Roger Staubach said of the first time the team saw the name. "We were labeled 'America's Team,' and the narrator said something about the Cowboys being 'the Notre Dame of professional football.' I thought it was a joke and they'd bring in the *real* highlight film next."

NFL Films said they drew the title from crowd scenes of games the Cowboys played around the country. Cameras recorded a large presence of Dallas fans in every stadium in the NFL. The idea of "America's Team" spun off "this display of national allegiance" to the Cowboys.

"After the '78 season, the Cowboys had just lost a crushing Super Bowl to the Steelers," Bob Ryan, the vice president and editor in chief of NFL Films said of the name. "I wanted to come up with a different twist on their team highlight film. I noticed then, and had noticed earlier, that wherever the Cowboys played, you saw people in the stands with Cowboys jerseys and hats and pennants. Plus, they were always the national game on television. If you think back, there has always been one team in each sport that has support from fans nationwide: the Yankees in baseball, Notre Dame in college football, the Boston Celtics in pro basketball. They are all America's teams. So I put that name on the Cowboys' film, and in 1979 the TV announcer for their first game introduced the Cowboys as 'America's Team.' They took a lot of heat for it, but it stuck. Other clubs, like the Atlanta Braves and the U.S. Olympic hockey team, have tried to call themselves 'America's Team.' But that name belongs to the Cowboys."

Tex Schramm could have vetoed the title because it was a blatant brag. Instead he embraced it, since the perception helped him promote the Cowboys as the number one team in the country.

Popular on the Hardwood as Well

"By 1978 we could tell how much the Cowboys had become a part of America's culture," Drew Pearson said of the team's overall popularity around the country. "We could feel it. Everywhere we went people wanted to be part of the Cowboys, people wanted to identify with the Cowboys. When we went out of town to play away games, airports, hotel lobbies were always packed with Cowboy fans, and it had been that way in previous years, but it was really peaking, really out there. We knew from the type of endorsements some of the players were getting, the type of appearances players were getting, we knew by the reaction of this city, anywhere we went we were known, and we were treated as special individuals.

"Our popularity was at an all-time peak, and it wasn't just in Dallas. It was on a national basis. I was running the Cowboy basketball team at that time, and we would go all over and sell out not just gyms but arenas.

"We played the Pittsburgh Steelers up in Pittsburgh, and 9,000 people came. We played a group of all-stars in San Antonio in the HemisFair Arena, and 10,000 people were there for that game. So we understood our popularity and what success and winning had brought to us, and we liked, it. We wanted to keep it going."

The Name Evokes...

What did the name "America's Team" do for the Cowboys? In the big picture of the NFL, what does it mean to be loved and hated more than any other team?

Cowboys defensive back Cliff Harris said, "We were the clean-cut team. It's because of Roger. They developed his image because that's what he was—Captain America."

"I hated 'America's Team,'" quarterback Danny White said. "It became bulletin-board material for every team in the league. PR people didn't have to go out on the field and face those other guys."

"When I first came to the Cowboys, I felt like I was becoming part of a legend," Randy White said. "I mean, they had always been winners, far back as I can remember. It was kind of special, thinking about the Dallas Cowboys, and them making me their first draft choice."

On the other hand, Howard Cosell summed up many fans' feelings about America's Team, at least those not in Texas, saying, "The Cowboys are the most overrated, overhyped team in professional football."

chapter 9

A Blue Star and a Hole in the Roof

Silhouetted by light from above, Bill Parcells watches his team warm up before the start of a game against the Tampa Bay Buccaneers on Thursday, November 23, 2006.

I don't know why we always wore white jerseys at home. I don't know where it came from. I mean, hell, I was just glad to have a jersey.

—Walt Garrison

I'll Take Cotton Fields, Please

I really liked the Cotton Bowl. I played there five years before the Cowboys moved to Texas Stadium, but I didn't realize that I liked it as well as I did until the team moved. And Texas Stadium was nice, don't get me wrong. At the time it was state of the art, the fanciest stadium in the NFL. Not the biggest, but the fanciest son of a bitch. It had all the big, luxury suites and the Stadium Club.

But here are the differences: the Cotton Bowl had the blue-collar guys from right off the midway, the fans who went to the fair, drank a few beers, and then would go to the game. They'd buy their tickets in the end zone and sit there and holler and boo and do whatever. And like I told somebody one time, people went to Texas Stadium not to make the scene, but to be seen. They sat on their hands. Hell, a lot of them were too good to clap. They wanted to sit up in the suites, or they wanted to sit on the 50-yard line and wear the finest clothes that money could buy and come prancing in. So the fans at Texas Stadium weren't as good, on the whole, as the people who went to the games at the Cotton Bowl.

Now, they're still fans at Texas Stadium, don't get me wrong. They are dyed-in-the-wool, hard-core fans, just like in the days at the Cotton Bowl. But they're all in the upper deck, because that's the only seats they can afford. I remember when the Cowboys first started at the Cotton Bowl, I never did go because I was a Texans fan. I used to go to the Dallas Texans games, and they sold more tickets than the Cowboys. And if an adult bought a ticket, they'd give two free or something like that. You could bring your kids in for nothing and sit in the end zone.

Texas Stadium was a nice place to play, but the field, I didn't like the field. The Cotton Bowl field was a lot better. That Tartan turf that they put in at Texas Stadium—I think that's what they called it—was harder than a brick. It burns you a lot more when you slide on it. The field at the Cotton Bowl was a little softer, and when you're falling down, a little softer helps a lot. –W.G.

NFL Stadiums

I loved to play in Washington at RFK Stadium because the crowd hated us—just flat-out despised the Cowboys. San Francisco was always fun because when you were out in Kezar Stadium, the fans would pour beer on you and stuff. It's great to play in places that have great fans. Denver was always fun to play in because the fans in that old stadium, Mile High, were just six feet behind us. All you had was a barbed wire fence between you and those fans. I think playing in Philadelphia was good, old Vet stadium, but they hated us more than any other city. The Giants weren't as bad. We played in Yankee Stadium my rookie year, and then we played in the Yale Bowl while they were building Giants Stadium. Playing in the Yale Bowl was like we were in a high school game. We were out there in a little aluminum kind of building off the field. And I'm not sure, I might have made this up, but I think we might have gone back to the dressing room at halftime, but it sounds better if you tell people we just met in the end zone like the high school kids always did.

Wrigley Field had part of the end zone in the bleachers. You could actually buy a ticket and sit up there and catch a pass. A guy could actually catch a pass and land in a seat and be in bounds. And those places were...you never think about them when you're playing in them...I mean, there's a statue of Babe Ruth out there in front of Yankee Stadium, and that's kind of cool. And Wrigley Field, it probably didn't mean anything at the time, but you tell people that you played in Wrigley Field and they say, "Oh my gosh!" So we played in a lot of the old stadiums. We played in Pittsburgh before Three Rivers was built.

Cleveland was probably the worst place to play in the world because the field was always muddy. It was always damp because it was right there by Lake Erie. With the lakes up there, the humidity is always about 140 percent and the field was always bad. Buffalo was a bad place to play. I don't remember the name of that old stadium, but the turf, it looked like one of those polo matches where the horses throw up big chunks of turf. Well, that's the way

Buffalo was. I think they just laid that sod down and it didn't have any roots. –W.G.

The "Arlington" Cowboys

That is just so stupid. I mean they didn't even let the people vote on when and where the new stadium should be. I thought that this was a democracy, but evidently not. The city of Arlington and Fort Worth made out like bandits in getting the new Cowboys stadium. Fort Worth loves the fact it's not in Dallas. The new stadium will be closer to them than it is Dallas—a lot of people are mad at the city of Dallas. And they're not going to stay over there. They're going to Cowtown, they're going to Fort Worth to spend their money and they'll stay in Arlington. The stadium is right in between Dallas–Fort Worth, actually, right next to the baseball stadium. And I don't think you could have picked a better location. –W.G.

Where's Tonto?

It was before a preseason game against the Rams in L.A.—we were at the Coliseum—and they had us lined up for the pregame introductions of the players. The offense was being introduced that day; I guess we won the flip or something. Anyway, we're lined up and ready to run out on the field. I was looking over the field, looking at the crowd and some of the other pregame fun they were doing. And that's when I spotted the Lone Ranger, Clayton Moore the actor, sitting on Silver in another tunnel. As strange as this seems, I got excited and went over and introduced myself to him.

The Lone Ranger has always been a big deal to me. I've been a big Lone Ranger fan forever. After introducing myself to Clayton Moore and talking for a second or two, I came back and got in line. Coach Landry said, "Walt, you need to get in line and pay attention to what's going on." And I said, "Coach, that's the Lone

Ranger and this is just an exhibition game." I thought it was more important to shake hands with the Lone Ranger, who I'd never met and might not have ever met, than stay in line for introductions to a meaningless preseason game.   –W.G.

Just for God

It was supposed to be the best stadium ever, and maybe for a few years it was. Texas Stadium was everything Clint Murchison wanted it to be. The inner workings of the facility were carpeted, escalators were always handy, and then there was the concrete canopy to keep all spectators dry in case of rain—the football field-size opening in the roof. Murchison believed football should be played outside—indoors.

The stadium was supposed to be domed, but the structure could not support the weight of the entire roof. And, more important, public funding ran out before the roof support structure could be modified. This resulted in most of the stands being enclosed, but not the playing field itself, a common structure trait used in European soccer stadiums.

"We could easily have closed up the hole in our roof," Murchison said. "But I don't like watching football in the Astrodome. Our fans are protected but can still see the sky. We haven't totally closed out the elements. But because of the competition of television, you have to cater to customers as they have never been catered to in the past."

Texas Stadium cost about $35 million dollars. Prospective season-ticket holders had to purchase a bond at either $250 or $1,000, depending on the location of the seat they wanted. There were 65,000 seats and 158 suites in Texas Stadium when it opened, and the 16 by 16-foot suites cost $50,000 each and seated 12 at the going rate for season tickets.

It was built to make money, and it did.

The players developed different feelings about the new stadium. They often felt like ancient gladiators who maimed each other for the pleasure of spectators lounging in elegant comfort. Said tight end Billy Truax, "The whole place is weird. You're down there on the field, and you know they're up there. It's like the lions and the Christians all over. We'd better keep winning. Thumbs up is better than thumbs down."

Thumbs up or down, Cowboys linebacker D.D. Lewis coined the most famous quote about Texas Stadium. "Texas Stadium has a hole in the roof," Lewis said in 1982, "so God can watch his favorite team."

Silver and Blue

After spending the first four years of the franchise's existence in blue and white uniforms, the Cowboys made a radical change—and major upgrade—to their Sunday best.

"I liked Green Bay's uniform, with the gold pants," Cowboys GM Tex Schramm said of the team's uniform change in 1964. "Then I saw Georgia Tech. They also had gold pants, but they had a real good-looking white jersey with the numbers on top of the shoulder pads rather than on the arms. I thought that look was terrific. I copied Georgia Tech for the Cowboy uniform.

"The metallic color was a new color. The manufacturers had to make a new dye with new materials. It was a unique color that became associated with the Cowboys. The new uniform was a big deal in the image and popularity of the Cowboys; it was classy and original and people loved it."

Jerry's World

What else would you expect from America's Team? It has been dubbed Jerry's World, but the real "working title" of the structure hardly inspires awe and wonder—Dallas Cowboys New Stadium. The price tag for the future home of the Cowboys does inspire something—if not awe, then bewilderment. Originally estimated to cost $650 million, the stadium's construction costs surpassed $1 billion, making it one of the most expensive sports venues ever built.

"I'm convinced it's a building that will be a classic," Cowboys owner Jerry Jones said of his new stadium's design. The monster-size tab is worth every penny to the billionaire Jones.

"No doubt about it, I want our fans to have the pride in a building that is recognized in a quality way," Jones said.

The building plan is certainly impressive, with the glass exterior its most eye-catching feature. Jones said the glass is made to glow blue and silver during the day, then the colors will reverse at night.

"It's basically a changing color scheme, but all within the traditional colors of the Cowboys," he said.

Retractable glass doors on the ends will provide an open-air feeling on days when weather permits. Jones anticipates that for most games the roof will be closed and the ends open.

"Really, truly, it is the front door," said Bryan Trubey, principal designer for HKS Architects Sports & Entertainment group. "Jerry and his family insisted on making a civic entryway." The new stadium will accommodate 80,000 fans, with the possibility for expansion to 100,000, and will be ready for the start of the 2009 NFL season.

"The challenge for us with this new stadium was to innovate, but at the same time never forget to acknowledge tradition," Jones said. "This new stadium embodies the spirit of the Dallas Cowboys, and that starts with the familiar hole in the roof."

The best feature? The exterior of the stadium is designed to cast off a silvery tint, just like the team's helmet.

chapter 10
Jerry's Team

Jerry Jones takes questions in December 2006 while standing in front of an artist's rendering of the Dallas Cowboys–proposed $1 billion stadium in Arlington, Texas.

I want to own the Cowboys for the rest of my life. I want to manage the Cowboys for the rest of my life. And when I die, I expect my family to manage the team.

—Jerry Jones

Football Today

Everything is different in the game today. The money, free agency, and the salary cap. Yeah, I think that's the biggest thing. A third of the team changes every year because of either the salary cap or somebody's offered them more money or whatever. So what you have is a nucleus of probably 15 or 20 players that stay there, and the rest of them change. The fans end up rooting more for a uniform than for a person. When I played, they could tell you who Bob Lilly was and Lee Roy Jordan and Roger Staubach and Craig Morton and Dandy Don. They knew them by heart 'cause they saw them every week and every year, year after year after year. There were so many players, just like me, who played their entire careers for one team. And I think that would be the worst thing in the world, to get traded; but sometimes it works out well.

Mike Ditka probably would have never gone to the Super Bowl, or Lance Alworth with the San Diego Chargers, or Bobby Joe Conrad, who played with the St. Louis Cardinals. They wouldn't have had an opportunity to go. –W.G.

Another Okie State Alum

The thing was that Jimmy Johnson coached at Oklahoma State, which is where I went to school. Then he left and went to Miami. I didn't particularly like him because he left my school. He kind of turned the program around at Oklahoma State there a little bit and then he left. I don't blame him, I mean it's a bigger school, bigger recruiting, and more money and all that stuff, you know. But what you don't understand is that when I retired, I retired. I didn't keep up with the Cowboys. I didn't care.

Does that make any sense to anyone but me? I didn't keep up with Jimmy Johnson or Jerry Jones or anybody else. I didn't have any feelings one way or the other. I could have cared less who they got for a coach. I mean, I want to see them win, but as far as...I mean they had Chan Gailey and Barry Switzer and Jimmy

Johnson, I mean those things didn't change my life one way or the other. People can't believe that I don't watch football today. I enjoyed football when I played, but I just don't watch it. I'd rather go ride or something—ride horses, rather than stay inside on a nice afternoon and watch football. –W.G.

Good-Bye Walker

I couldn't see what the hell Minnesota was thinking to trade seven draft choices for one guy, but then I couldn't see how or why Ditka, when he was the head coach in New Orleans, traded all his draft choices for the right to pick Ricky Williams. Same deal. But I thought it was a hell of a deal for Dallas to get all those draft choices for Herschel Walker. And Herschel was a great player, but when you get three first-round picks and several other draft choices for just one player, it's probably a pretty good deal. Let me restate that: it's probably a great deal for one team and stinker for the other. And that's the way it was. –W.G.

The Wildcatter

He was just your average millionaire oilman who happened to love football. Jerry Jones was deep-sea fishing in September 1988, in Cabo San Lucas, Mexico, when he read in a day-old San Diego newspaper that Dallas Cowboys owner H.R. "Bum" Bright was looking for a buyer for the team he'd bought in 1984. Jones, a former Arkansas Razorback defensive lineman (and cocaptain of the 1964 national championship team) made a call to Dallas. The pieces fell into place pretty fast, and by the spring of 1989, he had bought the team. He beat out dozens of other bidders that included, among others, Los Angeles Lakers owner Jerry Buss, a Japanese group, and even a group fronted by Roger Staubach. The deal was sealed on February 25, 1989, and for the tidy sum of $150 million, Jones became the owner of the Dallas Cowboys.

While he played well in Dallas, the Cowboys parlayed "The Trade" of Herschel Walker to the Minnesota Vikings into a Super Bowl dynasty.

Jones wasted little time in making his mark on the team. With Tex Schramm at his side, he helicoptered to an Austin golf course and told Tom Landry that he was no longer the coach of the Dallas Cowboys, a move that labeled Jones as The Man Who Fired Tom Landry. He didn't care. Jones brought in his old college roommate Jimmy Johnson, head coach at the University of Miami, to replace Landry, a move that would produce three Super Bowl trophies.

Herschel Heads North

On October 12, 1989, the Cowboys sent running back Herschel Walker to the Minnesota Vikings in the largest player trade in NFL history. Combining the players and draft picks they received with a keen eye for talent and a little bit of luck, the Cowboys ended up with three Super Bowl trophies, while the Vikings were left clinging to nothing but a pipe dream.

This was the deal: believing Walker was the missing piece to his team's championship puzzle, Vikings president Mike Lynn acquired the Cowboys running back for five roster players and, most important to Dallas, a variety of draft picks.

"We did not want to send Herschel to any team not competing for the playoffs and Super Bowl," Jimmy Johnson said. In actuality, the Cowboys were asking the moon for Walker, and the Vikings were willing to pay. Still, Walker had to accept the deal, and he hedged at the beginning.

"Everyone said Herschel was holding up the trade because he wanted this and that and more money," Walker said. "But that was not true. I was waiting to see what the Cowboys would do. They did what they thought was best for the Dallas Cowboys, and I did what I thought was best for Herschel Walker."

Jerry Jones said the deal was completed when he agreed to pay Walker "exit money," reportedly $1.2 million. Walker was in the fourth year of a five-year contract that paid him $1 million a season.

Troy Aikman, Emmitt Smith, and Michael Irvin were at the core of the Cowboys' championship teams from the 1990s.

Walker was never used properly by the Minnesota coaching staff, and he left for Philadelphia soon after without ever leading the Vikings to a Super Bowl. Dallas, meanwhile, parlayed their new assets into several starters on their championship teams, including Emmitt Smith, Russell Maryland, and Darren Woodson. In a final twist, Walker ultimately wound up back in Dallas, rejoining the team in 1996.

Super Blowout

Even though the lopsided score was easy to see, Jimmy Johnson said the obvious, anyway.

"I felt like we had the best football team," said Johnson. "When you turn the ball over as many times as they did, you'll have trouble. Sometimes it snowballs."

The Cowboys had just humiliated the Buffalo Bills 52–17 to win Super Bowl XXVII.

"You never in a million years think about scoring 52 points," Cowboys offensive coordinator Norv Turner said. "But they turned the ball over nine times, so that's what can happen."

Jimmy Johnson and Cowboys owner Jerry Jones hold up the Vince Lombardi Trophy as they celebrate Dallas's 52–17 victory over the Buffalo Bills in Super Bowl XXVII in Pasadena on January 31, 1993.

"In our division, you play Philadelphia and the Giants and Washington twice a year," the Cowboys' Jim Jeffcoat said. "We gear up there. You can't play us soft, because we will go right at you."

"We play tough football in the division," James Washington, the fifth-year Dallas safety said. "It prepares us when we get out of the conference. They tried to pound the ball on us and went nowhere."

"I just tried to keep everything in perspective and stay calm, especially with all of the pageantry and excitement that was around me," said Dallas quarterback and Super Bowl MVP Troy Aikman. "My first Super Bowl experience couldn't have been any better, because we spent the week practicing at UCLA, so I was very familiar with my surroundings."

"We didn't know what to expect, and I thought it would be a tough ballgame," said Dallas running back Emmitt Smith, who rushed for 108 yards on 22 carries. "Things started working out for us. They turned it over and we took advantage of the opportunities."

The Cowboys finished with an embarrassing 1–15 record in 1989—and now they had earned another Lombardi Trophy.

"There was never any doubt we'd get to this point," Johnson said of his team's overwhelming win. "The concern was how long it would take."

"When you're taken in the first round as a quarterback, especially when you're the first player taken, your only purpose is to win a championship for the team that drafted you," Aikman said. "So there's a real sense of fulfillment because you did what the franchise drafted you to do.

"I always believed we'd win a Super Bowl in Dallas. That didn't mean it was going to happen, but when it did, it didn't really come as a surprise."

"In my wildest dreams, I never thought about winning a Super Bowl," James Washington said. "Where do you go from here? You try to repeat."

Silly Rings

While all three Super Bowl wins in the 1990s were special to the Cowboys' players, the first one over Buffalo is just a little bit higher on the emotional satisfaction ladder.

"That was the first of three titles we won in Dallas while I was with the team," tight end Jay Novacek reflected in *Super Bowl Sunday* on the 52–17 win over the Bills. "All three championships are close to the top for me. Super Bowl XXVII, our first one, is so much bigger emotionally because we were so doggone happy to be there. It's an incredible feeling. The second one was a challenge, just because few teams have ever won back-to-back. And then the third one was something that we proved to ourselves. We were older, more mature, even though some people didn't act like it (myself included). We proved that we could still win; that we still had that desire.

"Knowing that I was a part of three Super Bowl championships with the Cowboys is an incredible feeling. I don't necessarily concern myself with the Super Bowl rings we received. In fact, I always call them 'stupid rings.' I've never worn them. My normal response when someone asks me about them is to say that I traded them in for a good horse. A surprising amount of people who know me well enough evidently kind of believe that. Everyone knows we won those Super Bowls, so why do we have to show off the ring?

"Obviously playing in those Super Bowls is something I will always remember. Now, whenever January comes around, I know what type of seasons those postseason teams have had. I know what it takes in terms of mental preparation to win a playoff game. There were times when I played and the playoffs basically meant extra money to us. It's really more than that. Once you start winning those playoff games and you start getting closer and closer to the Super Bowl, it's a heck of a lot more than just playing for money, it's playing from the heart."

Shaking It Up, Moving Forward

It was before the 1994 NFL draft, and Jerry Jones was address-
ing several college seniors who were anxious to find out what their
future would be in the NFL. They circled the Cowboys' owner and
listened to him speak.

"How lucky I am, how lucky we all are to be a part of the NFL,"
Jones said. "Some of you may, indeed, become Dallas Cowboys.
We are very happy to get this chance to get to know you better.
But wherever you may wind up, we wish you all the best. And if
you become a Cowboy, you'll get a chance to become part of
something very special. You know, there's nothing like being a
Dallas Cowboy."

Who was Jerry Jones in 1994? There were many opinions, but
it was generally agreed that he was an egomaniac, a self-centered
owner who craved attention. It was also agreed that he was a
dynamic, forceful owner who contributes his all to his team and
league.

"Change in life is a given," Jones said in a 1994 interview.
"Don't confuse change with a lack of respect for tradition. You
want to do something to harm tradition? Refuse to change. I'm
just passing through, like we all are. The Dallas Cowboys are
bigger than me, and they will be here longer than me or you. Tom
Landry and Tex Schramm and Tony Dorsett and Roger Staubach?
All great for the Cowboys, but now all gone. This franchise has a
legacy of winning and championships and of having visible management. It does not have one of visible ownership. I accept that
and people having difficulty accepting that change.

"The Cowboys are unique. Tex was unique. He was a core and
spirit of the Cowboys. He was visible, active. The Cowboys
became part of his persona, and he became part of the Cowboys'
persona. Well, there's your blueprint. It is one I believe in."

"I share the responsibility for the relationship not working out,"
Jones said of the split between he and Jimmy Johnson, who left

Barry Switzer smiles as he hoists the Vince Lombardi Trophy after his team beat the Pittsburgh Steelers 27–17 at Super Bowl XXX in Tempe, Arizona, on January 28, 1996.

the team in 1993. "Things were getting tense here. You had people walking on eggshells. You had people in meetings afraid to speak up and take a side on an issue because they were afraid of being at odds by appearing to side with Jimmy or with me. But through all of that, we made decisions together. We worked together, and I'm proud of what we accomplished.

"Some people told me, 'Well, all you've got to do is stroke Jimmy and everything will work out.' I had every confidence in Jimmy, and there was no need to do that, I felt, because he had a 10-year contract. In the early part of our relationship, the owner never came to a meeting, it was just Jimmy and Jerry. In the end, when free agency arrived and the salary cap and the landscape changed, the owner had to come to the meeting, and that became the problem. The owner had to stay and the coach had to go."

"This has been and will be a 'we' program," Jones said. "The instincts of trading, of moving up and down in the draft, is related to my business experience. [Johnson's successor] Barry Switzer knows people and he knows football talent. We've got the best staff in the NFL, and I agree that two heads are better than one. But six or seven heads are better than two."

"I had success in the oil and gas business and I wasn't a geologist," Jones said. "I had success in the poultry business and I wasn't a farmer. I know enough about football to respect and adhere to the recommendations of the people who have done their homework. I know enough about football to know that people count and to be on the same page with them. I know enough about football to involve everyone and put them on the line so that they have some stake in the future."

"It's his project, his business plan, his team," fullback Daryl Johnston said. "We understand that."

"When we first heard rumors about the change, we said no way, that things here are already too good to be true," linebacker Darrin Smith said. "And then it happened. And so the question now is if we can win without Jimmy. We can. Jerry has our support. We don't even talk about it much now."

"I'm going to keep the flame broiling underneath the fire," Jones said. "I have energy that is now being redirected. My dad once told me not to ever write a check that my fanny couldn't cover. Some of my best days have come with me squarely behind the eight ball."

Barry Support

When Jerry Jones and Jimmy Johnson parted ways, it could have been a bad transition when Barry Switzer took over as the team's new head coach. Two of the Cowboys' top players, quarterback Troy Aikman and running back Emmitt Smith, tried to help with the transition shortly after Switzer took the job.

"I think Barry is an outstanding coach and the transition should be smooth," Aikman said. "I believe he will do a good job. He's keeping the same staff. We're keeping the same offense and defense. I think we'll be comfortable with what he's trying to do."

"I talked to Jimmy and he was very positive and upbeat," Smith said. "He said Jerry treated him well with his contract. If Jimmy is satisfied, I'm satisfied.

"There is no need for me to moan and groan. I have to make the best of the situation and keep moving. I understand he's a player's coach, and you don't have too many like that."

Many thought there might be animosity between Aikman and Switzer because the quarterback transferred away from Switzer's Oklahoma program. Not so. "He was very helpful getting me to a university to do what I do best," Aikman said of Switzer.

While Aikman and Smith were ready to work with Switzer, the Cowboys' other top offensive weapon, Michael Irvin, was still upset over the departure of Johnson. When asked if he would play for Switzer, Irvin responded with a resounding "Hell no!"

"He'll learn to deal with it," Emmitt Smith said of Irvin. And he did, as the Cowboys won their third Super Bowl in four years, in Switzer's second season as head coach.

Bye Bye Barry

At the end of the 1997 season, Jerry Jones said good-bye to Barry Switzer, who had resigned after a four-year tenure as head coach of the Cowboys.

"Very simply, Barry Switzer was the right man for the right time," Jones said of Switzer. "And under his tenure he was able to help us achieve three division titles, two appearances in the conference championship game, and one world championship."

Jones called the resignation an "emotional and difficult" decision but concluded it was time to "chart a fresh new path." He said the standard for Switzer's successor would remain the same.

Bill Parcells brought his considerable reputation, and ego, to the Cowboys in 2003.

"I believe that we will be able to field a team that will be very capable of challenging for a Super Bowl berth," Jones said.

Switzer, in a written statement, thanked Jones for giving him the opportunity and agreed it was time for a change.

"My desire to see this team have success is my only priority," the statement said, "and, at this time, I believe a fresh start in this position will give the Cowboys their greatest opportunity to return to the top."

And so the coaching merry-go-round in Dallas continued: Chan Gailey for two seasons, Dave Campo for three seasons, and Bill Parcells for four years.

And no more Super Bowls.

Troy Aikman and Rayfield Wright at Canton

Inducted into the Pro Football Hall of Fame on August 5, 2006, Troy Aikman and Rayfield Wright are two of the 14 players who played for the Cowboys to be honored by the Hall. Parts of their induction speeches follow.

Troy Aikman's Hall of Fame Induction Speech

Thank you very much. I'd like to first of all say that I'm very pleased to see all the people who have stuck around here today. I know it's been a long day. I know it's hot. I know a lot of you have come to watch other inductees and have reason to leave, but you stuck it out, and I appreciate that very much.

I'd also like to say that the people in Canton, Ohio, have been absolutely terrific. Over the last three days we've been here, the hospitality that they've shown myself and family has been nothing short of spectacular. I look forward to many return trips to the Canton area in the future years. I don't anticipate missing many Hall of Fame weekends. Thank you for the hospitality and thank you for the courtesy you've shown me and my family.

It's said you're judged by the company you keep. If that's true, I'm in great standing today. It's an honor to be a member of a Hall of Fame induction class that includes five men for whom I have such admiration and respect. Warren Moon, Reggie White, Harry Carson, and Rayfield Wright played the game the way it should be played. John Madden coached the game the same way.

I would have loved to have had any one of them on my team.

I, too, am saddened by the absence of Reggie White, an amazing player and even better man who left us far too soon. Reggie, Warren, Harry, Rayfield, and John represented the game with class, just as Lesley Visser, the first female recipient of the Pete Rozelle Award, brought respect and professionalism to the field of journalism for her work in print and broadcasting. It makes me proud to be in their company today.

I'm also honored to have Norv Turner here today as my presenter. Norv was my coach for three years. That's it. I started playing football at the age of seven and retired when I was 34. Of all those years, Norv and I were together for only three. Yet there's no doubt in my mind that if Norv Turner had not entered my life, I wouldn't be joining these men in the Pro Football Hall of Fame today.

He meant that much to my career and to the Dallas Cowboys. Norv came to Dallas as an offensive coordinator in 1991, my third season, and turned around one of the worst offenses in the National Football League, and gave guidance to a young quarterback who was in desperate need of some direction.

We went to the playoffs that season, and over the next two years won back-to-back Super Bowls. At a time when coaches are guarded about getting too close to their players, Norv proved you could be both a great coach and a great friend. Yet it's our friendship that is most special, because it has endured long after he stopped coaching me in Dallas. He's the big brother I never had. And I thank him for having the biggest single influence on my career. Thank you, Norv. I wouldn't be here without you.

When I was a kid, all I ever wanted to be was a professional athlete. It wouldn't have happened without the help of a lot of great coaches. I was blessed to be coached by some of the game's best, beginning with my earliest years of junior All American football in Cerritos, California, with the Suburban Hornets....

Then of course there was Jimmy. Jimmy Johnson and I arrived in Dallas the same year, 1989, both fresh from college, both eager to prove ourselves. Didn't take long to see that Jimmy was unique, and it wasn't just because of his hair.

What struck me most about Jimmy was his fearlessness. Some coaches play not to lose. Jimmy always played to win. Some guard against overconfidence. Jimmy insisted on it. Jimmy's boldness set the tone for a young group of players who didn't know much about winning but were eager to learn. Jimmy was the right coach at the right time for the Dallas Cowboys, and I'm grateful to have been given the opportunity to play for him.

I was also fortunate to have played for a franchise whose owner was as committed to winning as anybody on the field. Every move Jerry Jones made was done with the sole purpose of helping the Cowboys win championships. That's what he was about then, and still is to this day.

As a quarterback, the player who more than any other is ultimately judged on his ability to win, I couldn't have asked for anything more from an owner. It was a privilege to play for Jerry and the rest of the Jones family, and I appreciate the opportunity they gave me and their commitment to making the Cowboys a championship organization. Thank you very much.

In addition to great coaching and ownership, I had the pleasure with playing with a very gifted and special group of players. It's no wonder we enjoyed so much success in the '90s considering all the talent we had. I enjoyed the best seat in the house as I watched Emmitt Smith run his way to the NFL's all-time rushing record. Michael Irvin, whose work ethic was second to none, was one of the most special teammates I've ever had the opportunity to play with.

I always took great pride in being a part of the triplets with Michael and Emmitt. There were so many other special players that I had a chance to play with, guys such as Jay Novacek, the irreplaceable and unsung hero of our franchise, Daryl "Moose" Johnston, the blue-collar guy who I'm not ashamed to say was better at his job than any other player on the team was theirs, including myself....

In Dallas, my role as the quarterback was to move our team down the field and score points. Sometimes that meant passing the ball, sometimes it meant handing it off. We had a good system in Dallas. Although it wasn't one that allowed me to put up big numbers, that was fine. I did what was asked to help the team win. So it is extremely gratifying that after a career of putting team accomplishments in front of personal achievement, today I am receiving the greatest individual honor a football player could ever receive....

In closing, I'd like to share something that a close friend used to tell me back when I was playing. He'd say this when times were tough, maybe we'd lost a close game, I'd thrown the deciding interception, or the grind and the rigors of the season were beginning to take their toll on me. What Norv Turner would say was this:

"Sometimes we have to remind ourselves that these are the jobs we've always dreamed of having."

Norv was right. For as long as I can remember, all I ever wanted was to play pro sports. A lot of kids want that, but very few actually get the chance. I was able to live a dream. I played professional football. That I was able to do so with so many great players and coaches and win three world championships and wind up here today with all these great men in gold jackets, well, it's almost too much to believe. I am humbled to be welcomed to the Pro Football Hall of Fame, and I thank you.

Rayfield Wright's Hall of Fame Induction Speech

First of all, I'd like to give praise and thanks to our father in heaven and through his son, Jesus Christ, that has given me the ability to play sports.

I learned a poem in the eighth grade entitled "The Road Not Taken." It's about two roads. One was well traveled, the other was grassy and wanted wear. Through this poem, I discovered that life would give me choices. It was recognizing those choices that proved to be the greatest challenge. Looking back, my instinct was to always take the easy road. But the easy road never came my way.

You see, I grew up in Griffin, Georgia. My mother and my grandmother raised me, my brothers, and my sister. We didn't have much money or any luxuries to speak of. Times were tough, and I recognized at an early age the struggles that we faced....

During my college years, I excelled in both football and basketball, but basketball was still my preferred sport, as I averaged over 20 points a game, 21 rebounds per game. In fact, the Cincinnati Royals tried to sign me my junior year to come and play basketball for them, but I declined that invitation because I needed to stay in school and get my education. And I did just that.

And I knew I was headed for the NBA. But, again, I found myself traveling yet another road. My senior year, I received a telephone call from a gentleman by the name of

Mr. Gil Brandt of the Dallas Cowboys. He stated that the Cowboys were interested in drafting me. I asked him, "For what?" I had my sights set on the NBA.

But I realized that potential, playing for the Cowboys, was a God-given opportunity, and I couldn't ignore it. I decided to attend the Cowboys' training camp, which was in July. The Royals' camp didn't start till August. I kind of figured that if I didn't make the Cowboys team, I could go right to the NBA.

That year, 1967, the Dallas Cowboys had 137 rookies in training camp. Gil Brandt was signing everybody that could walk. Only five made the team that year, and I was one of the five.

I thank you, Mr. Brandt, for giving me the opportunity to play for the Dallas Cowboys.

My career started as a tight end. Don Meredith was our quarterback at the time. Recently I asked Don, I said, "Don, you remember throwing me a touchdown pass against the Eagles?" He laughed and said, "Rayfield, I wasn't throwing the ball to you, you was just so tall, you got in the way."

Two years later, Coach Landry called me into his office and said, "Rayfield, I'm going to move you to offensive tackle." I looked at him and I said, "Coach, I never played that position before in my life." He said, "I know, but you're quick, you learn fast. Besides, we got a young quarterback coming to the team this year, and his name is Roger Staubach, and he don't stay in the pocket. He runs around a lot, and he needs a little bit more protection."

But I was never one to question the authorities of elders. Coach Landry, I believed in his decision, and that was good enough for me.

Now, offensive linemen are taught to protect the quarterback the same way that the Secret Service protects our nation's president. In this case, Roger Staubach was our president. The director of the Secret Service was our offensive line coach Jim Myers. He built an offensive line that was unmatched. And today I cannot accept this honor without bringing Coach Myers and his offensive line into the Hall with me. That line consists of John Fitzgerald, Tony Liscio, Dave Manders, Ralph Neely, John Niland, and Blaine Nye.

Gentlemen, I'm proud to call myself your teammate. I share this enshrinement with you.

And to our defense, you were the Doomsday. I'm thankful that I only had to face you guys in practice. I remember Coach Landry once telling me, "Rayfield, no matter how many awards or accolades you receive, you will be never greater than the team." The Dallas Cowboys were a team, and what a team the Cowboys had during the dynamic decade of the '70s.

I have 13 years of players and coaches I'd like to acknowledge today. But I've been told that I'm not to go into overtime. We had a lot of shares of playing games in overtime back in the glory days. You can understand the pressure that I face up here right now.

But we played together as a team in 12 playoff games, five Super Bowls. Guys, you know who you are. I know who you are. The Cowboy fans around the country know who you are. I always remember that we were winners, and I treasure those moments and memories.

Fans always ask me who my toughest opponent was, how tough they were, who they were. I played against the best. My body still hurts when I hear their names called. But I wouldn't be here today without these great players. Deacon Jones, thank you for your gracious welcome into the NFL. In case you're wondering, Deek, the answer is yes, my mother knows I'm here....

I've had many mentors in my life who always said, "Let honor and success come to you only if it's deserved, not because it's sought after." Being enshrined today is, indeed, an honor. I extend my gratitude to the selection committee for nominating me, with special thanks to Mr. Rick Gosselin of the *Dallas Morning News*. Some say that patience is a virtue. After 22 years of eligibility, God knows that I'm not a saint, but I am a Dallas Cowboy. And today I acknowledge my 2006 inductees. I'm privileged to be in such a stellar class. I would give thanks and shout to our troops who are protecting this great nation. May God keep you safe. To thank everyone who is playing and who has played a vital role in my life would take me 60 years, so I'll try to keep it brief.

I wish to tip my helmet to the Dallas Cowboy fans, especially the ones who remember my playing days and America's Team of the '70s. To the Bob Hayes family, I thank you for your support and continued support over the years. To my former teammates, the ones who are here today, to those who have reached out to me over the past several months. I love you guys, and I thank you....

To every young athlete within the sound of my voice, it takes courage to dream your dream. Don't let them sit in the locker room. Take a leap of faith. Listen to your parents and respect your elders. Learn from your successes and your losses. Defeat is possible and is a challenge to do better next time. Be satisfied you gave the game everything that you had, and remember this: don't be afraid to travel the road less traveled, because Larry Rayfield Wright did, and you can, too.

May God bless you, and may he keep you, and may his countenance shine down upon you and give you peace. God bless you. I love you.

Tuna Time

A coach with a history of success joining a team with a history of success. But what about the future? The coach was Bill Parcells, who ended his three-year retirement from coaching in 2003 to rule the Dallas Cowboys sideline. Everyone expected his comeback to return the team to glory.

Bill Parcells was confident. "We can't fail," he said of his new team. "We have to be successful. I'm hopeful I can bring the Dallas Cowboys another championship. I'm ready for the pitfalls and the land mines. I have been around the block a few times. I think I can avoid trouble most of the time."

"I love football. He loves football," Cowboys owner Jerry Jones said of his new coach. "I've made a lot of mistakes. You know I have. I am not going to grow careless with this relationship. If he fires me up, I hope I can do the same with him. We are going to make this work."

"We must win. We will win," Jones said. "Winning is the name of the game."

As for coming out of retirement? "Football is what I am and what I do," Parcells said.

In his book *The Final Season: My Last Year as Head Coach in the NFL,* Parcells wrote about how he coached a game against the Cowboys and was surprised to find Jones on the field.

"Hey, it's his team," Parcells wrote. "He can do anything he wants with it. That's his prerogative. But I don't see any good it can do for him to get involved in the coaching end of the game. None whatsoever. I know he's a great marketing guy, one of the best in the history of the league, and he knows how to make money with his team and his stadium.

"If an owner wants to come around during the week and encourage the players, root for them and let them know he is with them, that's fine with me. But once the owner wants to coach, then I'd be out of there the next day. I couldn't coach in that situation myself. That should not be his domain."

"Will I be allowed on the sidelines?" Jones asked. "Yes. It's my sideline."

"I'm okay with pretty much everything," Parcells said. "I'm an employee of the Dallas Cowboys. We have an owner in place. We have entered into a partnership. We will work in concert. We both want to go to the same place."

60 Minutes of Bill

"I think confrontation is healthy, because it clears the air very quickly," Bill Parcells told Mike Wallace on CBS's *60 Minutes* in 2004. "And most of these athletes that you deal with are pretty well used to that kind of thing."

Players taking a swing at the Tuna? "Oh, yeah," Parcells said. "We've had a few of those. That's okay." Parcells said that he never used a confrontation with a player to make an overall point.

"These things happen," Parcells said. "I don't have to make examples out of players to establish my own place. I don't feel like I have to."

"You mean everybody knows what a prick you are?" Wallace asked.

"Yeah," Parcells answered with a laugh.

The strangest part of Parcells's coaching prowess is that he hasn't enjoyed his successes. "Someone kinda helped me with that recently, and he said that, 'The gift you have is also your curse,'" Parcells said of the misery the game brings. "'And then, when you get at a certain place, you're looking for something else that challenges you even greater. And as a result, you become miserable until you find that.' It was never called to my attention so specifically."

"It's difficult to explain. But this game and this business is not without a myriad of incessant problems," Parcells said. "Even when you're successful, even when you win the game, about an hour after the game, you have a litany of things that you now have to deal with that are problematic. So the times that you are happy are minute compared to the time that you're dealing with problems."

Then the big question: why did he come back for more misery after just three years of retirement? "I was just starting to get a little bit bored," he said. "That thing that's always reached out to me, to bring me back, it's been a long arm. It's a tentacle. It gets you, and it drags you back in."

The long arm belonged to Jerry Jones, the Cowboys' owner.

"I was basically perceived as someone that was difficult to work with," Jones said on the show. "That it was difficult for coaches to do their job. I am involved, was involved hands-on. The expectations that I place on what we do as a team, and I know our fans are expecting, those can be very nerve-racking.

"I work hard at making this work. And I've involved our entire organization in a way that makes this a good experience for him. I'm tempted to use the word *pleasant*. But you can't use that word in football."

"You know, the end is near. I really do know it, you know what I mean," Parcells said of his remaining time in football. "So I can enjoy it more. I'm enjoying it a lot more now than I did, and I'm not beating myself up quite as much."

Taking a T.O.

He actually knew what was going to happen. And when the problem needed to be taken care of, it wasn't going to be Jerry Jones, any of the other coaches or players, or even Terrell Owens himself who would take care of things.

"At the end of the day, I knew when we acquired this player that I was going to be the one that had to deal," Bill Parcells said of his talented yet wildly unpredictable wide receiver. "What anybody else thinks, present company included, anywhere nation-wide, all those chatterboxes, I don't care. I'm going to do what I think is best for the Dallas Cowboys. Whatever opinion anyone else has is totally irrelevant to my line of thinking, because they don't have all the facts and I do. I consider things that you people don't even think of. The only thing that's tedious to me is having to talk about it all the time."

"Players need to worry about themselves, their jobs, and what they're doing," Parcells said. "I'm sure they're observing what I'm doing. There are some who have been with me that know, and then there are others that are going to have to learn."

"If that's one of his rules, that's something I have to abide by," Owens said just before the start of the 2006 season. "I think everybody is trying to make this into me versus Bill, or Bill versus

Terrell Owens celebrates a touchdown against the Atlanta Falcons during a December 2006 game.

T.O. I wouldn't say our relationship is where it needed to be, but I think it's a building process for both of us. We don't know each other very well."

And they never really did during their one season together with the Cowboys.

To T.O., It's a Good Thing

Not everyone was saddened by Bill Parcells's retirement following the 2006 season.

"I am just hoping his retirement brings promise to what the team has to offer," Owens said. "This past year was a big letdown. On paper we were as good as anybody we played against every week. The end result didn't show that. Our play was not indicative of what we could have done; what we should have done. Hopefully, the owner will hire a coach to take the team to the next level."

T.O. even said that Parcells fostered an unhealthy environment for the players on the team.

"Sometimes change is good," Owens said. "I think it was needed."

Apparently Parcells didn't talk to Owens following his accidental drug overdose at the beginning of the '06 season; T.O. said the Tuna didn't talk to him for weeks afterward, and worst of all, failed to offer any words of encouragement that would have been welcome.

"Coming into this season and this situation, I wanted to be positive," Owens said. "When I talked to him for the first time we left an impression on each other. I still think he is a great guy. But he is like my grandmother. You love the person, but they are stuck in their old-school ways. You can't move them from their way of thought."

"Parcells's coaching style hurt us. You don't know who is doing what," Owens said. "You don't know who is calling plays. That is why our offense was up and down. You saw that at the end of the year. It filtered off. We as a team felt the frustration. I felt the frustration. But Bill is Bill."

Owens admitted that he did not play up to his potential, but he also said that he didn't fit into the offense.

"I was underutilized in the offense," Owens said. "A new coach can be good for the Cowboys. It's not just me. But my teammates know I could have done more. I wasn't used as a number one receiver. If you don't involve a guy, that person is not going to be as productive as he can be. That's how I felt."

So T.O. was talking again—can that really be a good thing?

chapter 11
Moments and Other Memories

Dallas Cowboys owner Jerry Jones speaks with Tex Schramm Jr., former president and general manager of the Cowboys, at a news conference in April 2003 where Jones announced that Schramm would become the 12th man inducted into the Dallas Cowboys Ring of Honor at Texas Stadium.

I really enjoyed playing football. I used to look forward to Sunday like you look forward to a big party. I loved it. There ain't nothing like a Sunday from the time you wake up until the time the game's over. The dopeheads can take whatever they want, but they'll never get that kind of high.

—Walt Garrison

Hanging 'Em Up

Retirement is an individual thing, and nobody can tell you when to retire. Most football players know when to retire. When Don Perkins, our great fullback throughout the 1960s retired, he actually played in the Pro Bowl his last year. Why would he retire? How could he retire? He did because for him, it was time. No matter what you do, sooner or later, you get fed up with the process of playing football. This might sound strange to some people, but there are other things in life besides the game.

You can't play football until you're 65.

When you have an opportunity that pays you more than playing football, you retire. That's why it never surprises me whenever anybody retires because it's a personal thing. Players know when they've lost that deal inside of them that makes them want to play—that thing that gets them up in the morning and makes them think about football 24 hours a day, seven days a week for six months out of the year. You might think about what you did wrong and what you can do better. And you go over plays and you study plays and you study defenses and you study, study, study. I studied more with the Dallas Cowboys than I ever studied in college. Because it's a different game. But nobody can tell you when to retire. It's a personal decision. So it doesn't surprise me when anybody retires because, number one, it's none of my business, and there's a lot of extenuating circumstances that come into play, whether it's a good job, whether it's your wife doesn't want you playing anymore, your kids don't want you to play anymore, your folks or whatever—that's a personal thing. –W.G.

My First and Last

I don't remember the game much or who we played. I just remember being in the locker room or being in the meeting room before we went to play with Bob Lilly and Don Meredith and Don Perkins, Dan Reeves, Lee Roy Jordan and Chuck Howley and Dave

Edwards and Ralph Neely, guys that I'd been watching two or three years on television and hearing about them. And then there I am in the same locker room with them—I was amazed.

"What the heck am I doing here?" I thought to myself. I mean these are great professional football players. Why am I here? And that was my first recollection of pro football. You could give me a million dollars and 20 guesses and I probably still couldn't guess who we played. The fact that I made the team was the big thing.

Now, I very much remember my last game. We played Oakland and got beat—it was the final game of the 1974 season. But I didn't know it was my last game. Why? I didn't know I was going to tear my knee up bulldogging in the off-season. I didn't plan to retire, and I would have probably played another year, maybe even two, if I had not had to have a knee operation in the off-season because of rodeo. I hyperextended it and tore all the ligaments and stuff.

But I was lucky. U.S. Tobacco offered me a job in the off-season, and I couldn't see holding onto a job that was coming to a close real quick or starting a new one. So I didn't even think about it and called Coach Landry.

"Hey Coach, I'm done. I'm going to retire," I told him. He said "You thought about it?" I said, "Yes, sir." And he just said, "Okay." He knew. I mean he played football, too. Like I said, it's a personal deal. Can't nobody talk you into it or talk you out of it. It's something you do. You know personally when it's time to retire. A lot of players hang on, they know they should have retired two years before they did, but they *have* to hang on. I couldn't do that, and I didn't.

And when I got off the phone with Coach Landry, I called U.S. Tobacco and accepted their offer. –W.G.

It's All in the Head

There was one game I played in where I had two concussions. I don't remember a thing about the game, and the funniest part of it is that it was one of the better games I ever had in my life. On the

Tuesday after the game when they were showing the films, I'm looking at it and I don't remember any of the plays. It's like you're watching somebody else play. Usually when I watched the film on Tuesday I could remember every play. But that day I couldn't.

So I got one concussion and went out, and then they sent me back in because it was still in the first half. But I don't remember anything about the whole game. Evidently I was sitting on the sidelines and Coach Landry said, "How you doing?" And I said, "Fine." So he said, "Go on in." Okay, I went in and got another concussion. I had a total of five concussions when I was playing, and out of nine years, that's not bad.

A concussion is a strange thing. They all knock you out—you're really unconscious, but you're not out. I mean you're not out cold. The worst thing is you just don't remember anything, you know. And they make you puke. I remember that—you throw up. A concussion makes you throw up.   –W.G.

The Pain of It All

Now, I don't like pain. But they say some people have a low threshold and some have a high one. Evidently, mine is high. They used to ask me, "Doesn't it hurt?"

Goddamn right it hurts!

Everything hurt. I'd have bruises all over me when a game was over. It looked like an army walked on me. Considering the beating I was supposed to have taken, I came out of football pretty good. But I don't think I probably got hit as hard as some other running backs. And that was my game—taking a hit. I used to think nobody could ever hurt me no matter how big they were.

Then I found out that was bullshit too. I got broken ankles, broken ribs, broken collarbones. But, luckily, I never had to miss a game because of those injuries. Actually, the worst injury I had was a pinched nerve. Every time I stood up I got dizzy. So I missed three or four games because I couldn't do anything without falling on my ass.

There is a difference between pain and injury, and some players couldn't distinguish the difference. Football players play in pain. That's the business. If you play football, you gotta play in pain. That's why I don't think I'd enjoy playing today. It's changed so much. Guys are making so much money. They're not hungry. It hurts a little bit, they take the day off. −W.G.

Rivals

Anytime you play within your division it's going to be a rivalry game. Washington and Philadelphia were our biggest rivals because we played them twice a year. St. Louis, the St. Louis football Cardinals, weren't as big a rivalry because they weren't as good most of the time. I guess George Allen had a lot to do with the Washington rivalry. And Philadelphia had the fans who were terrible to the opposing teams, really bad for visiting teams. Those two probably stood out more than any of the other teams we played, because we played them twice a year.

It's important to remember that a rivalry is only good when both teams are good. Sometimes we played when Washington was down and it was easy to beat 'em. That wasn't really a rivalry. And sometimes, they beat us. But when it was a rivalry, when both teams were fighting for the division lead, it was always fun playing in RFK, the old stadium up there. Their fans hated us, absolutely loathed the Cowboys, which made for some great games.

The fans in Philadelphia were great. Bad, but great. I wish Dallas fans were more like Washington and Philadelphia fans or even Denver. The Broncos had great fans. San Francisco had great fans. You'd come out on the field in San Francisco and they'd pour beer on you and stuff like that.

Dallas fans, I think for the most part, don't care if the Cowboys win or lose, because when they moved from the Cotton Bowl to Texas Stadium it became more of a social event than a football game. If you were there, if you had good seats or you had a suite or something and were a little more important than other people, that's what it was about. —W.G.

Tex

Tex Schramm joined the Cowboys at the time of the team's inception in 1960. Twenty-nine years later, the architect of America's Team stepped down following the firing of Tom Landry.

With a list of accomplishments spanning all of pro football, Schramm was an advocate for wild-card playoff teams, instant replay, and other innovations we take for granted today, such as a referee's microphone, a 30-second clock between plays, extra-wide sideline borders, wind-direction strips on goal posts, and multicolor striping for 20- and 50-yard lines.

In 1991, Schramm was inducted into the Pro Football Hall of Fame in Canton, Ohio. NFL Commissioner Pete Rozelle was his presenter.

"I first met Tex Schramm in 1952," Rozelle said in his introduction speech for Schramm.

I interviewed with him for the Los Angeles Rams' public relations job. So Tex explained what was wanted for the job and so forth. We had a good discussion and finally we got to salary. He said the salary would be $5,500 a year, and I said I thought maybe $6,000 would be more appropriate, and so we compromised on $5,500. So that set the stage for my obvious appreciation of Tex's negotiating skills. They came into play again some 14 years later, in 1966, in the merger of the AFL and the NFL, when, largely because of my appreciation for his negotiation with me, he became the point man for the NFL in negotiating with Lamar Hunt in the merger....

But his big break came in 1960 with an expansion team in Dallas, Texas. Tex became the president and chief executive officer of the club for Clint Murchison. His first step was to hire a relatively obscure defensive coach, assistant coach, for the New York Giants, named Tom Landry. And, as you know, he, too, came here to this building. Tex and Tom were a tremendous team for 29 years in Dallas, Tom taking care of the team on the field and Tex taking care of everything else. They had a tremendous record. They were known as America's Team. Tex didn't name them that, but he kind of clung to the tag anyway. They had 20 straight winning seasons. Eighteen of those were in the playoffs. And they participated in five Super Bowl games, winning two of them. The amazing thing is the three they lost—I'm sure each one of them bothers Tex to this day—by a total of 11 points, those three games they lost in the Super Bowl.

He did other things in Dallas. He elevated the level of club operations for the whole league. He developed computer scouting to help him on the draft. He had a very colorful Cowboy newsletter every week. He developed a tremendous state-of-the-art stadium in Dallas. He also built a tremendous Cowboy complex of offices. Of course, not forgetting maybe the most important thing, my wife will take exception to this, but the Dallas Cowboy cheerleaders weren't too bad either....

In any event, I can only say that 160 men have been inducted into this Hall of Fame, none with more pride, more appreciation, or more happiness than Texas E. Schramm. I give him to you today.

Schramm took the microphone and addressed the crowd.

Thank you, Pete. What years. What memories. So many contributed. So many that I wish I could start naming them, but if I did, Jan Stenerud would never get up here to the rostrum. But the great players, and I think two of them really epitomize what I would like people to think of, are

Roger Staubach and Bob Lilly. They're here in the Hall. Our coach was Tom Landry, a very, very unique person, because he not only was a great football coach, but he stood for so much more. And when he was on that sideline, I think it just gave everybody a sense that there was some solidity and some reason in this world. Tom was the only coach we had. That was all we needed. The only head coach. But he was backed up by a bunch of great assistants as is anybody that's successful.

One of them who was with us just about the whole trip, our defensive coordinator, a member of this Hall, here this weekend, Ernie Stautner, from Pittsburgh. Great person. Great name. And another, Jim Myers. You folks don't know him, but he was with us for 20 years, 26 years. He was our offensive line coach and worked in that area. One I'm very pleased of was one of our younger coaches. In fact, we had two younger coaches I'm very proud of. The other one is here this weekend and that's Dan Reeves, who was a player and a coach with us. And the other one is that fella who always stays in the background and you really don't ever hear very much about him because he always…he likes to be low key, Mike Ditka.

Now, at this point I want to tell you specifically the three men that are most responsible for me being here. The first one, he's gone, Dan Reeves, not the coach. He was the farsighted owner that moved the Cleveland Rams to Los Angeles in 1946 before anybody else was thinking about going to the West Coast. And he hired me in '47, and he was a very innovative, forward-thinking, bright man, and he gave me the first base to build on with the Los Angeles Rams. I'll always be indebted to him.

The second one is probably just about more important or as important as any of them and that was Clint Murchison Jr., who was the founder of the Cowboys. He had the courage to go with an expansion team and he had the courage to go with me as his general manager. He gave us tremendous support. I think he would be proud today that I am here, because I wouldn't be if it weren't for the rare confidence and unqualified support that he gave to all of us in the Cowboy organization.

Now, the third man, and I want to give you just a little…when I was with the Rams in 1947, I was 26 years old and there were 10 teams in the league. It wasn't really a national league then, in 1947. They were all [grouped] into the northeast part of the country. There were two New Yorks, two Chicagos, Green Bay, Detroit, Philadelphia, Pittsburgh, and Washington, and Los Angeles stuck out on the West Coast. I learned very, very quick that before any club can be successful, or any individual can be successful, the league has to be successful, because the teams and the individuals get their recognition and their strength from the strength of the league.

So, early on, I made up my mind that I wanted to try to play a role in the development of our game, development of our league. If necessary, a club has to sacrifice for the good of the league. And I'll tell you how they thought a few years ago, which I'm not sure applies now. But if you got a picture today of a team in New York City, like the Yankees, just to make it…agreeing to share all their television revenue with all the members of the league, that's what the Wellington Maras did in 1961 for the good of the league. That was a breed, a special breed of people. And in working with the league, the reason I said that this man had so much to do with me being here, because if it had not been for Pete Rozelle, I don't think that I would have been able to make any of the contributions or played any of the roles that I played.

Finally, this is something really important to me, because in my role there's nothing like the fans. The fans, they're just a great bunch of people. I talk to them every week on the radio. The fans, they develop an attachment that is very close to love like you have in the family. Boy, they love you when things are going good and when you disappoint them, you know, then they want to lash back. But that's because you always want to…so often you hurt the one that you love the most. And so the fans, they will always be a tremendous part of my life. I love you all.

To recognize the depth of this honor for me is, I've been the league for 40 years, starting in '47, the people that are here in this hall are people that I saw and met and I never dreamed that somebody on the administrative side like myself would ever be here. They were my heroes. They were people that I idolized and now it's really staggering to think that here I am joining them. There could be no greater honor. I'd also like to hope that maybe because I'm

Roger Staubach's game-winning 50-yard Hail Mary pass to Drew Pearson in the December 1975 playoffs against Minnesota helped build Staubach's legend.

standing here now, some of those people that are out there doing those jobs that you never hear about in the organization, will think, "Gee, now maybe I have a chance." But I'd like to give them one little piece of advice. You have to remember that the game is the thing that has to progress. The game is the thing that has to grow and if you dedicate yourself to making sure that the game grows, instead of your own career or your own team, you'll find out some amazing things will happen for you. I thank you. I'm humble. And I'm telling you that I'm the happiest man in this organization.

The Hail Mary

The game wasn't supposed to be close, but the cold, shivering Minnesota fans didn't seem to mind. There was only half a minute left in the game, their beloved Vikings were ahead, 14–10, and about to win this divisional playoff game. Dreams of another Super Bowl appearance had to be running through their minds.

And then Roger Staubach said a prayer while he threw one.

Unleashing a bomb at the end of the game was about the only option for the Cowboys. Minnesota had stifled their offense most of the day, and the Cowboys were in desperation mode.

"I closed my eyes and said a Hail Mary," Staubach said in the locker room after the Cowboys' victory over what was arguably the best Vikings team ever.

"I was looking for the ball out and away, and I felt I had one more gear to get past Nate [Wright, Vikings defensive back], but then I saw the ball was underthrown," Drew Pearson said. "Nate was running at an angle a little in front of me to cut me off if the ball went deep. But I came back with my arm in a swim move, reaching over Nate's shoulder for the ball. I was as surprised as anyone in that stadium that I caught that ball."

The Hail Mary pass was born.

Just 24 seconds remained, and moments later, Dallas ran off the field with a 17–14 playoff win.

"When I threw it, I actually underthrew it a little bit, because I pumped and then I turned to throw," Staubach said of his pass. "Drew had taken off down the sideline, and he actually came back and caught the thing underneath his arm."

"Nate Wright fell on the play, and they said I pushed him," continued Pearson. "You know, there was contact. When I brought my arm around, there was contact. And that might have been what knocked him off balance. But there was never, ever any deliberate push or anything of that nature."

"After I threw the pass I got knocked down," Staubach said. "It was an away game, and when I didn't hear any screaming, that was good. And then I saw some objects coming on the field. I thought they were flags, but they were oranges the fans threw on the field. The Super Bowl was in the Orange Bowl that year. I guess that's why they had the oranges there."

The win sent the Cowboys to Los Angeles to play the Rams in the NFC Championship Game—Dallas destroyed L.A. 37–7 to win the conference.

"That play is what people associate Drew Pearson with more than anything," said Pearson. "That play labeled me as a 'clutch' receiver, labeled me as 'Mr. Clutch.'"

It was also the play that cemented Staubach into his rightful place among the greatest quarterbacks of all time.

The First Thanksgiving

A couple of Thanksgiving Day traditions are easy to take for granted—most people will eat some turkey and then watch the Dallas Cowboys win a football game. And while it seems the Cowboys have been playing on Turkey Day forever, once upon a time there was a "first time," and that first time turned out to be a mighty important game.

On November 24, 1966, Dallas played the Cleveland Browns at the Cotton Bowl in a game that figured to decide who would win the NFL's Eastern Division. The Cowboys had yet to win anything in their short existence—they had no big-game wins and little big-game experience.

"I can see why some people say we couldn't win the big one," Don Meredith said of his team after the game. "But the players never think about it that way. It's something built up by the sportswriters. We haven't actually been in a position to play the big-game before."

They won this one.

A total of 80,259 Cowboys fans jammed the Cotton Bowl and saw the Cowboys handle a Cleveland team they had lost to earlier in the season. Dallas played solid, fundamentally sound football and, with the help of Danny Villanueva's four field goals, defeated the Browns 26–14.

Don Perkins ran for 111 yards and a touchdown, but the day really belonged to Meredith, whose leadership and poise led the way. He hit 16 of his 24 attempts for 131 yards and was seldom in trouble.

"Don was tremendous," Landry said of his quarterback, "as good as I've ever seen him. He called the best plays of his life. He kept changing our formations and keeping the Browns off balance."

The win put the Cowboys' record for the year at 8–2–1 and virtually clinched a spot in the NFL Championship Game. It turned out to be quite a Thanksgiving in Dallas—and now all Thanksgivings in the Big D are special.

"We just beat 'em," Ralph Neely said of the Cowboys' effort. "Nose to nose all the way. No big plays, no flukes. We just beat 'em."

"That victory over the Giants in the final game last year was a big one, because it put us in the Playoff Bowl," Landry said. "But this one is our biggest victory against a formidable opponent. A win like this matures a team. It matures you a little more each time until you win a championship."

Success

It was a long time coming, but Mel Renfro, possibly the best defensive back to ever wear a Cowboys uniform, was finally inducted into the Pro Football Hall of Fame in 1996.

Renfro led the NFL with 10 interceptions in 1969 and finished his 14-year career with 52 picks. He also returned three kicks for touchdowns and was named to the Pro Bowl 10 times.

"The Cowboys were probably great because of their consistency, with Coach Landry and the way they played the game [and had] 20 consecutive winning seasons," Renfro recalled of the team's winning ways. "I was able to play in eight NFC championship games over a period of 14 years. The consistency, you know they didn't have the big moneys or the free agencies, so players had a tendency to stay on one team. I think there was a lot more loyalty. Nowadays with the different contracts and the rules and the free agency, players are moving around so you can't...you don't have that consistency or dynasties. That's unfortunate, but you know, that's the way the game has changed.

"Still it doesn't take away from the game itself. It's a great game and I think that the Hall of Fame does a great job in representing those great players in that great game."

The Last Comeback

Nobody knew it at the time, but on December 16, 1979, Captain Comeback fought his last winning battle, leading his team to its fourth straight NFC Eastern Division title. Roger Staubach threw a perfect alley-oop pass to Tony Hill for the final points needed to pull out a nail-biting, stomach-churning, come-from-behind 35–34 victory over the Washington Redskins. There were 39 seconds remaining on the game clock when Hill crossed the goal line.

Staubach's overall game performance was brilliant, as he connected on 24 of 42 passes for 336 yards and three touchdowns. It was also the 21st time he had guided Dallas to a fourth-quarter win and the 14th time he'd turned defeat to victory in a game's final two minutes. Washington was leading 34–21, had the ball, and was driving with just under four minutes left in the game.

"What can I say about him?" Tom Landry said of his veteran quarterback, "Roger is simply super in these kinds of situations. He's done it before and knows he can do it."

"There was," Staubach said, "an electricity that was going on out there in the latter stages. We just never quit. Even after their early 17-point lead, we managed to get a lot of momentum going and came back."

Unbeknownst to the crowd, his teammates, his coach—even himself—the game was the last hurrah for the 1963 Heisman Trophy winner. Dallas lost a heartbreaker to the Rams in the first round of the playoffs two weeks later, and Staubach decided to hang up his blue-starred helmet after that.

"The story is, if Coach Landry would have let him call his own plays, or if he would have given him more leniency in calling his plays, he would have continued to play, but Coach Landry wouldn't let him do that," Pearson said of Staubach's retirement. "I had a lot of influence on Roger as a teammate, and being his receiver, I could have probably begged him or coaxed him to come back, but I didn't. I pulled back. In that type of situation you have to let the player make his own decision.

"I couldn't even go to his press conference, because I didn't want the whole world to see me crying and broken up. I did watch it on TV and I watched it with nothing but tears in my eyes and sadness in my heart, because I didn't want to see him go. It was tough to take, but as always in life, it goes on and you have to keep moving."

chapter 12
Two Men

*Tom Landry and Roger Staubach
face the media in the week
leading up to Super Bowl VI in
New Orleans in January 1972.*

To me, Tom Landry is the greatest
coach in the history of the game.

—Roger Staubach

The Hall

I've actually only been to Canton one time. We played a preseason game there against Chicago in 1968. They rotate the Hall of Fame game around for different teams. I know the induction ceremony is nice and the men who have had great, great careers deserve all the accolades they can get, but I never seen it, not in person.

Rayfield Wright invited [me] to come to his induction at Canton—the first time I ever got an invitation from anybody—and I wanted to go, but couldn't. I did call Rayfield the morning they inducted him and told him I was very proud of him and that I wished I could have been there. –W.G.

Landry and Staubach

Coach Landry is an absolute Hall of Famer. He was a great player at New York, a great coach at New York, a really great coach at Dallas. There was no way they could have kept him out of the Hall of Fame. And Roger was a great player, an exciting and great player. He won a lot of games. He's the one who brought back the two-minute offense and got people to watch the offense the last part of the game. Roger was like a lot of great quarterbacks. But the one thing about him was that he just didn't lose. When Roger was the Cowboys' quarterback, he never lost a game—he just ran out of time.

Roger never thought that we could get beat. That's just the way he felt. But as far as both of them going into the Hall of Fame, I think Coach Landry did a lot for the NFL. He played defensive back and coached with the Giants. And Roger of course did so many great things. I can't think of anybody else I'd rather have the ball in their hands at the end of a game other than Roger except maybe Joe Montana. –W.G.

Landry on the Importance of Winning

"I don't believe in winning at all cost, if that means cheating or doing things that are wrong," Landry said in a 1974 interview. "But if you think winning is not too important, then you are not willing to pay the price to win. Take away winning and you've taken away everything that is strong about America. If you don't believe in winning, you don't believe in free enterprise, capitalism, our way of life.

"Our way of life means succeeding and you must win to do that. Today in America everything is let's be free, let's be ourselves. But that eliminates responsibility. If you have freedom, you must have responsibility. If you're going to have free enterprise—have a country like ours—you've got to win, got to pay the price, got to do the things that make our country progressive. Once you start moving away from that—and that's what we're doing in America today—sooner or later you're going to fail. You won't remain strong.

"This country is organized no differently from a football team. It's built on discipline, competition, and paying the price. Take away those things and you have chaos, weakness, and immorality, all the things that are taking place in America right now. So winning is important to America. It's got to be."

Together at the Hall of Fame

In the summer of 1985, Roger Staubach asked Tom Landry to present him for his enshrinement into the Pro Football Hall of Fame. Landry did so gladly. Five summers later, Staubach returned the favor and presented his coach, America's Team's coach, to the Hall of Fame.

Almost every coach will extend any personal successes he's enjoyed along to his players. Landry was no exception. But as much as Staubach made Landry a winner by leading the Cowboys to come-from-behind victories, division titles, and two Super Bowl wins, it was Landry's guiding hand and gut feeling about Staubach that helped make him a Hall of Fame quarterback.

The two definitely belonged together.

On August 4, 1990, Staubach introduced Landry to the large crowd in Canton as the great coach took his place alongside the other immortals from the world of professional football.

"Mr. Commissioner, Mr. Mayor, Hall of Fame committee, Hall of Famers old and new, and most importantly you the fans who came to our parade route this morning and cheer in our stadiums, it's a pleasure to be here today," Staubach said to begin the presentation.

And I want to update you on the score [Hall of Fame Game], the Browns are winning 7–3. We have been up here a little long. I think our bus has gone out of style over there, but it's been worth every minute of it and it's a privilege for me to be here on this important occasion on behalf of Tom Landry.

On the stage though, some memories were brought back that weren't all the best. Ray Nitschke knocked me out of my first game as a rookie for the Dallas Cowboys. And then there's Ham and Greene and Swann and Lambert and Blount and Harris; that's enough to ruin your day. I'll tell you that right there. I have had the feeling since I've been sitting there, that there's a handful of you out there that are not Cowboy fans. That's the Communists out there in the group, but it's a…you know, a little over 20 years ago a dream came true when I first stepped onto the field at Cowboy training camp as a rookie. Five years ago, another dream came true when I stood before you as an inductee to this great Hall of Fame. My dreams and those of my teammates were fulfilled because of the efforts of one very special individual. Today I have the honor of representing the players of the Dallas Cowboys in presenting Tom Landry into the NFL Hall of Fame.

You know, Tom Landry was able to put a football team on the field that won for 20 years in a row; it's unprecedented.

Staubach loosens up under the Superdome lights as coach Tom Landry watches in the background in New Orleans on January 12, 1978.

It's an unprecedented feat of the National Football League, and one I don't believe will be duplicated again. You don't do that by accident. You do that because you know the game and you're a fierce competitor. But I don't want to get into statistics in the brief few minutes that I have. I really wanted to try and capture the spirit of Tom Landry.

He's hard to classify, not someone that fits the typical profile of a football coach. In fact, some might suggest that he's a man of contrasts, someone whose public image doesn't always reflect his true character. For example, how can a nice soft-spoken man, known for his fashionable tailoring on the sidelines, become a legend in one of the most physical, aggressive, action-oriented sports in the world? To watch his demeanor both on and off the field you would never expect that he was at home in a world of split-second execution and violent collisions.

Folks might say that he's conservative, that he doesn't change much, and I guess there's some truth to that. He's a man of unwavering beliefs. His faith and his family have always been the foundation for his life. I guess if you know his wife Alicia, it was a marriage that was made in heaven, if you want to get corny about a marriage. These values give him the confidence and inner strength to be one of the most persevering, dedicated men I've ever known. The self-discipline he developed along the way helped him to maintain balance in his life through good and bad times.

He wanted to win as much as any human being or any coach or any player that ever played the game, but he could always put victory and defeat in their proper perspective. While he might be conservative in some areas, let's all recognize that he was one of the innovators and architects of modern football. Cowboy teams became famous for their ability to innovate. Tom was always on the leading edge. He perfected multiple offensive sets, motion and shifting before the snap. The Flex defense forced opposing teams to radically change their offenses when we played. The shotgun is now used by practically every team in the league. In the minds of knowledgeable football fans, Coach Tom Landry is recognized as a visionary who is always one step ahead of the crowd.

Those of you who have watched Coach Landry on the sidelines all those years might have formed an impression of him as impassive or unemotional. The media played it up quite a bit, but the truth is that despite that cool outward appearance, Tom Landry is one of the most sensitive, caring individuals God ever put on this earth. In a sport that is tough as football can be and Tom Landry is as tough as they can be, Tom's sincere desire to win was at the top of his list. But he also cared for the individual and the team and that's what made him a winner. He agonized over tough decisions.

You'll find that former players believe that Coach Landry made them better individuals. The high tribute we can offer is genuine respect. Tom Landry certainly earned that from the athletes he influenced in his three decades of coaching. He has also earned that off the field in a lifetime of giving and caring.

So there are the contrasts that I've tried to put together of the spiritual side of Tom Landry, conservative yet innovative, quiet but generous and giving. He might appear somewhat distant, but he is always warm, compassionate, and understanding. Which is the real Tom Landry? They all are. He is exactly what he appears to be. There is no pretense in his style, no false images to maintain. His genuine nature and goodwill make him standout as the individual unique in his time. Tom Landry defines the word *class*.

In one of my weaker moments, I called Tom "the man in the funny hats." Speaking for football fans across the country, we miss that image on Sunday afternoons. But we're thankful for the memories he has given us, for the grace and dignity he brought to our sport. He has touched all of us in a way few men could. I'm proud to consider him a friend. On behalf of all the players who have had the wonderful fortune to be coached by the very best, it is my pleasure to introduce Coach Tom Landry."

The old, great coach stepped to the microphone and addressed the crowd.

Thank you very much. "I should have worn my hat tonight or today and you'd recognize me if I'd had that hat on I'm sure. But you know they're taking bets on whether I'll show any emotion today and the odds are very heavy that I won't. But you know, they told me this was going to be a great experience for me and you know I have been here to introduce several players into the Hall of Fame and I thought I would handle it very well. But when you're on this side of it, it's a little bit different. It's really a thrill for me to be here and if I don't show emotion, it's all on the inside though.

It makes it a little bit special today to have Roger Staubach present me for induction into the Hall of Fame. I could talk for hours about Roger Staubach. Because he is probably…there's probably no peer for players who can win the game in the last minute or bring a team from behind as Roger did. When we show our highlight films, you can see what Roger has done for the Dallas Cowboys. And as he said, he's representing the players that I've coached through the years. There's some of them here. I see Bob Breunig out here; I see Ed Jones here. Drew Pearson's here, also Robert Newhouse in there, Jethro Pugh, all those great guys that played for the Cowboys. I know I missed some that are here. I think Bob Bruenig's here too. I'm just delighted to have them here and all the other fans that are here today as well. I would like to recognize the enshrinees for the tremendous job they did in coming. You know they're all the players; I'm a coach. It makes a little difference you know from a coaching standpoint to go in the NFL, though I wish I'd been a good enough player to go in as a player. Boy, that'd been super, but I wasn't unfortunately. I'm glad to be here though as a coach. I had the pleasure of coaching against all these guys or playing against them. I coached four Super Bowls against four of them in the time. I understand now why Pittsburgh beat us twice. Their whole team's going to be in the Hall of Fame before this thing's over with….

But as I moved into the Cowboys, the Dallas Cowboys, I had the real pleasure to have an owner by the name of the late Clint Murchison Jr., who was very special in our whole setup. Clint Murchison who took over the Cowboys in 1960 and who was with us until he passed away recently in there, he never once criticized me or second-guessed me in the whole time that I was with the Dallas Cowboys. I remember after the 1963 team, we had only won five games after four years in any one season. They called a press conference and I remember we went to the press conference and everybody said, "Well, Landry's gone." Well, Clint walked in and says, "I'm going to give him a 10-year contract." With one year left. Now that's loyalty and that's support. And I believe that Clint Murchison was probably the one person that enabled us to go 20 years with a winning season because he took the pressure off of me, he took the pressure off of Tex Schramm and took the pressure off the organization. That's what makes great teams and great dynasties.

Others in the Dallas Cowboys, Tex Schramm was a tremendous organizer. He contributed greatly to the NFL in so many ways. He was largely responsible for our organization. Gil Brandt who was the other one that came in at the same time.

Of course the last year has been a very, very interesting one for me. I got fired and I'm in the Hall of Fame all in one year. So you coaches always remember there's always good things at the end of the rainbow if you stick at it. But I think my coaching staff is another reason that we were very successful. I had coaches that coached with me for 29 years. Jerry Tubbs did. I had Jim Myers and Ermal Allen who coached with me for almost 25 years. I had Gene Stallings for 14 years. Danny Reeves came up as a player and went all the way through and coached for me, went on to Denver in there. Of course Mike Ditka did the same thing. He came to us as a player and now he's coaching the Bears. And all these guys were with me more than 15 years as coaches, and that's what made the Cowboys what they were.

I had a great time in the NFL. I think after the 40 years I've been in it, I've spanned the whole gauntlet from failure to success in the NFL. Because when we were back in the '50s with no television…I don't think I made over $5,500 in those days to play the game. But that's what it was all about. But I saw the merger, the marriage of television and the National Football League, and that was the greatest marriage that ever happened in the late '50s, because from that spawned the American Football League and expanded what we have today in the National Football League. I just hope that the National Football League will continue to build on the great foundation that has been created by the Rooneys and the Halases and all the rest and all these Hall of Fame guys because they've made it possible and I think the game will continue on. It's a great pleasure for me to come into the Hall of Fame. I never thought I would make it, but I'm sure glad to be here. Thank you very much.

Staubach on Growing

"My philosophy has changed since I've grown up, as I've gone into each period of my career," Roger Staubach said in 1974. "I like to compete, I like football, but I don't particularly like a lot of things happening in professional sports today. The attitudes, the overwhelming desire to make a lot of money. It becomes more of a business, and I guess it is a business. I do agree that things are based on winning and getting into the playoffs and doing well. That's what it's all about.

"Growing up, I think it's wrong for people in these youth programs to apply the ideals of professionalism to young kids. For them, playing ball should be strictly for fun. Competition is a great thing, but a youngster should be able to lose well as well as be a good winner. The emphasis shouldn't be on winning and on being first-string. Let them have fun, share in the team. At each plateau the idea of winning should become stronger. From high school to college to pro sports, it gradually builds up. Winning is the most important thing in pro sports, but at other levels a young guy should be able to accept defeat and still be a good competitor. It's tougher to lose in the pros. But that shouldn't be turned around to mean, 'Hey, this is the ideal way to approach sports.'"

sources

Burton, Alan. *Dallas Cowboys Quips & Quotes*. Abilene, TX: State House Press, 2006.

Dallas Cowboys Media Guide 2006.

Dallas Morning News.

Donovan, Jim, Ken Sins, and Frank Coffey. *The Dallas Cowboys Encyclopedia*. Secaucus, NJ: 1996.

Fulks, Matt. *Super Bowl Sunday: The Day America Stops*. Lenexa, KS; Addax Publishing Group, 2000.

Garrison, Walt. *Once a Cowboy*. New York: Random House, 1988.

Golenbock, Peter. *Cowboys Have Always Been My Heroes*. New York: Warner Books, 1997.

Gruver, Ed. *The Ice Bowl*. Ithaca, NY: McBooks Press, 1998.

Klein, Dave. *Tom and the Boys*. New York: Zebra Books, 1990.

Luksa, Frank. *Cowboys Essential*. Chicago: Triumph Books, 2006.

Meyers, Jeff. *Dallas Cowboys*. New York: Macmillan Publishing Co., 1974.

Monk, Cody. *Legends of the Dallas Cowboys*. Champaign, IL: Sports Publishing LLC, 2004.

The New York Times.

Perkins, Steve. *Next Year's Champions*. New York: World Publishing Company, 1969.

Profootballhof.com.

Sham, Brad. *Stadium Stories: Dallas Cowboys*. Guilford, CT: The Globe Pequot Press, 2003.

Shropshire, Mike. *The Ice Bowl*. New York: Donald I. Fine Books, 1997.

The Sporting News.

Taylor, Jean-Jacques. *Game of My Life: Dallas Cowboys*. Champaign, IL: Sports Publishing LLC, 2006.

Towle, Mike. *Roger Staubach: Captain America*. Nashville: Cumberland House Publishing, 2002.